THE VIOLENCE OF PROTECTION

THE VIOLENCE OF PROTECTION

Policing, Immigration Law,
and Asian American Women

LEE ANN S. WANG

Duke University Press *Durham and London* 2026

Project Editor: Bird Williams
Cover design by Frank William Miller, Junior
Typeset in Garamond Premier Pro and Peridot Devangari
by Copperline Book Services

Library of Congress Cataloging-in-Publication Data
Names: Wang, Lee Ann S. author
Title: The violence of protection : policing, immigration law, and
Asian American women / Lee Ann S. Wang.
Other titles: Policing, immigration law, and Asian American women
Description: Durham : Duke University Press, 2026. | Includes
bibliographical references and index.
Identifiers: LCCN 2025032024 (print)
LCCN 2025032025 (ebook)
ISBN 9781478033271 paperback
ISBN 9781478029823 hardcover
ISBN 9781478062028 ebook
ISBN 9781478094616 ebook other
Subjects: LCSH: United States. Violence Against Women Act of 1994 |
Women—Violence against—Law and legislation—United States |
Asian American women—Violence against—United States—
Prevention | Asian American women—Crimes against—United
States—Prevention | Asian American women—Legal status, laws, etc. |
Women immigrants—Legal status, laws, etc.—United States | Federal
aid to law enforcement agencies—United States
Classification: LCC HV6250.4.W65 W3675 2026 (print) |
LCC HV6250.4.W65 (ebook) | DDC 362.88082—dc23/eng/20251120
LC record available at https://lccn.loc.gov/2025032024
LC ebook record available at https://lccn.loc.gov/2025032025

Cover art: Tsai-Wei Yeh, *The Farthest Distance*, 2016. Eastern gouache
on paper, 70 × 128.5 cm. Courtesy of the artist.

This book is freely available in an open access edition thanks to the
generous support of the University of California Libraries.

In loving memory of our Luna II 🐾

Contents

Introduction

"They all want to save someone. . . . They come looking for the quivering victim . . . but my question to them is, first, do you know what you need to know about immigration law? Because that is what your client will need." These words were shared with me during an interview I conducted with PJ, an attorney in the San Francisco Bay Area who worked at a nonprofit organization focused on addressing gender and sexual violence in Asian immigrant communities. I was struck by the distinction PJ emphasized between saving and need. But as she shared interpretations of her work, this distinction became central to the struggle between herself and survivors, between survivors and the law, and among Asian American legal and social service advocates. PJ was grappling with differing political responses to the role of policing in their work with Asian immigrant communities. At the time, I interviewed and followed the work of Asian American attorneys, social workers, case managers, and community organizers who overlapped on the long road of care for survivors. I do not refer to care in the sense of a self-help commodity or a multicultural object utilized by state and nonprofit entities, corporations, and even law enforcement. I am referring instead to care as a relational practice, an organizing politics within the political genealogy of abolition feminisms; care within and across communities that pauses, listens, refuses, and creates without any singular solution, expectation, or exchange. Care solves no problem because our ability to practice care, for ourselves and others, is the long struggle, not the temporary solution.

All the advocates I spoke with struggled to practice care while working for an agency or organization entangled within the neoliberal politics of the nonprofit industrial complex. Some of this struggle emerged in their work with clients and coalitional community members. Often the center of this tension hinged on the role of law enforcement—deciding whether to cooperate with or assist in police work and having to communicate with federal immigration enforcement. Organizations often relied on federal funding that in turn required them to form loose or formal partnerships with local police agencies. Others were part of networks to serve survivors detained by Immigration and Customs Enforcement (ICE) agents after an immigration raid on businesses or residences. Sometimes police officers or ICE agents were coalition members in antiviolence networks even while these same agencies were deporting and detaining migrant communities. Advocates shared reflections of struggle with their own self; they had to translate and represent survivors as deserving of protection to the very agencies that sought to deport them. Further, stories often interpreted advocacy work as a struggle with the practice of translating to survivors what was expected of them by the law, emphasizing the need for a certain kind of behavior and responsibility by someone already experiencing harm and grappling to survive that harm.

I conducted several interviews with PJ, and we saw each other occasionally over a period of sixteen months. She often spoke at length about survivors who walked away. PJ's role as a legal advocate focused on the survivor's legal status, as just one of many needs for survival that other case managers provided through women's shelters, mental health providers, and medical advocates at hospitals and emergency rooms local to the San Francisco Bay Area. And in some cases survivors who were her clients were referred by local police or federal immigration agents; these cases posed a different set of challenges: "There is always the chance they [the client] will walk away.... Attorneys experience that.... Most women want help right away, and they need [it], and that's why they call ... but because of what the process requires ... it's frustrating.... But a lot of clients walk away. It's more common than you think."

As PJ spoke, her stories reflected the stakes for someone who wished *to stay*, the risk involved in navigating all the varying state legal and social service agencies that would allow one to stay, and also the cost of walking away when movement was already policed and monitored. For noncitizen survivors, the decision to come before the law can never be free of pressures related to immigration law or local policing.[1] Thus, organizing or advocating around gender and sexual violence for immigrants is always entangled with the enforcement of immigration law and its relationship to state violence.[2] In my view, the politics and social movements grown from abolition feminist thought provide a possible path to build frameworks that refuse the separation of interpersonal harm from the violence of wounds left by state structures and systems. Abolishing the reliance on punishment in our spaces, relations, memories, and practices is a move toward a different creation and can be world building. For me, that starts with a slow attempt to abolish not only the victim as a legal subject through which the law unfurls policing but also the victim inside our political practices. I interrogate legal protections designed for undocumented and immigrant survivors largely under the Violence Against Women Act (VAWA), a landmark federal statute that has been debated, celebrated, and also critiqued from within antiviolence movements for its restrictions against tribal jurisdiction, funding categories, immigration provisions, and its role in expanding policing over communities. How a nation-state rescues and saves reveals how it governs through its investments in settler colonialism, imperialism, criminalization, and prisons. This book is an attempt to build an abolition feminist approach to the study of gender violence, US immigration law, and policing and to explore what this means for contemporary Asian American feminist politics.

At the time of this book's writing, the incarceration of women in prisons has increased 585 percent in the past four decades. This is a direct result of federal and state resources to fund police presence in cities and neighborhoods; harsher sentencing laws that target Blackness; surveillance of those deemed to be threats to heteropatriarchy, whiteness, and capital accumulation; stricter parole boards; and racialized and gendered limitations to reduce access and eligibility for life-affirming needs. US policing overwhelmingly targets, and relies on, the punishment, death, and incarceration of Black communities. Most women incarcerated today are not white. Among women in the US, Black women face the highest rates of incarceration. And among girls, Native communities face the highest rates of incarceration nationally.[3] And even further, *survivors* of gender and sexual violence form the overwhelming majority of women in jails today. Over four-fifths of women in jails report experiencing sexual violence or intimate partner violence *before* prison or jail.[4] These statistical summaries highlight the relationship between gender and sexual violence and carceral institutions, certainly. But what feminist-of-color and queer-of-color critiques have sought to really emphasize is that interpersonal violence is not isolated from state violence and that state violences institutionalized by racial systemic structures such as policing, prisons, and border enforcement are already sites of gender and sexual violence.[5] Such critiques argue against the framing of the "violent individual" somehow abstracted from historical and contemporary structures of violence, and instead emphasize the racial and gendered political, economic, and legal conditions under which some communities live with violence. If survivors are criminalized and punished inside prisons and jails, then it is a fallacy that prison walls keep criminals on the inside to protect victims on the outside. This is the myth of the perfect victim, and as this book will show, the myth plays a role in the racial politics of the Asian American model minority myth.

Criminalization is racially disproportionate, but it is far more than that. The myth of a universal, color-blind, and gender-neutral victim reappears today in so many social policies and rights-based campaigns that themselves remain silent on the criminalization of Blackness, the racial logics that produce "good" and "bad" immigrants, the colonial structures that introduce sexual violence, and imperial humanitarianisms. Thus, legal advocacy practices that aim to utilize law are already part of the racial and gendered legal meaning making that is required to interrogate the bind between protection and punishment. We might consider advocacy to be more than logistical or merely practical under the cover of the political in part because advocates themselves are often simultaneously part of community organizing, creative practices, and movement building. Not all, but certainly many. In addition, the actual effort of advocacy—the *practice*—confronts systemic state violences and our relational politics in different and strategic ways. It is only when some attempt to protect the practice as a territory that state power is prioritized over the life chances and needs of those living with vulnerability. But it is also worth noting that a more complex view of advocacy or client service does not automatically give way to a radical potential somehow divested of systems and structures of violence.

In many states, migrants who face immigration-related problems are often first pulled in by local police because of non-immigration-related issues, such as when police respond to a domestic violence call at someone's home where the survivor is not a US citizen. The need for legal status is unavoidably tied to a need to be free of policing.[6] Some survivors' legal status can be completely dependent on having spouses or family members who are legal permanent residents or US citizens.[7] Dependency in this manner can exacerbate control and conditions of harm. Additionally, lack of legal status can often shade how police officers and immigration officers interpret narratives from immigrant communities: whether they can even speak as survivors of gender-based violence while also being understood as someone living without legal status or citizenship. Where and how immigrant women encounter police influences the way survivors are heard, seen, or measured to be worthy of certain kinds of material protection from the law. Who can successfully become a proper victim before the law, what plight must they demonstrate evidence of, and what is the pledge that they must make to be protected?

The original passage of VAWA in 1994 was largely invested in pro-policing agendas regardless of the ongoing punishment practices targeting Blackness, establishing public safety campaigns, and normalizing the carceral state domestically and through humanitarian rescue projects abroad. The growth of VAWA via white feminist pro-policing agendas invested in victim narratives advanced neoliberal policies and programs of this era. These voices dominated over Black-women-led and multiracial movement building both inside and outside prisons focused on addressing the intersections of gender violence and incarceration rather than relying on criminalization and policing.[8] Kristin Bumiller has shown that white feminist anti-violence lobbyists and policy makers created an "abusive state," and Leigh Goodmark demonstrates the troubling alignment between anti-violence movements and law enforcement which result in the emphasis on perfect victims.[9]

Three decades after VAWA's passage, forty-six sexual assault and domestic violence coalitions signed a statement calling attention to their role in white-led public safety agendas—which ignored and erased abolition feminist Black, women of color, and Indigenous feminist frameworks—and failed reform policies based in policing rather than care and healing.[10] Notably, statements like these emerged in response to the voices of abolitionist organizers during the 2020 global uprisings for Black lives against police violence and decades of *dis*service by state and federal social welfare agencies, health and mental health, housing, and education institutions.[11] Further, in response, social workers and scholars of social welfare argued that political calls to defund the police must also extend to historical and contemporary imbrications between social work and policing.[12]

To return to PJ's words, her emphasis was a call to turn our attention toward the constitution of the *need*. The legal nonprofit PJ worked with engaged not only with city and county agencies, police, and federal immigration officers regarding local-level politics but also with Asian American–serving community groups, youth, and student volunteers across the Bay Area. In our interview PJ's reflection about "everyone" questioned not only the politics of state agencies but her own communities, political coalitions, and the competing stances on police within contemporary Asian American politics. That is, for PJ, a distinct difference emerges between the liberal humanitarian desire to rescue and the more material condition of a need. For immigrant survivors, those needs are specific and involve the already enforced and policed pressures of maintaining or obtaining legal status in the US and a tension endemic to the need itself, often satisfied by the law's production of a social difference among those who are deemed worthy of receiving that need and those who are not. In other words, *legal violence* is not the state of being excluded from receiving something of need; rather, it is the forced inclusion and enforcement as a subject on which a need is imposed to begin with. We might consider this to be the opposition between care and protection, or the opposition between a relational care versus "settler care," as Chris Finley has argued.[13] It is not merely the absence of a material resource that constitutes violence in one's life but also the presence of that need to begin with, particularly when the need is enforced through racial and gendered hierarchies.

PJ continued to describe how women frequently began a legal process and then walked away from it, given the considerable cost, time, and risk. With these few words, she described the broad landscape of legal practice—where humanitarian contradictions of rescue, success, and failure come together to negotiate racial identity, violence, sexuality—all while having to work within a state-sponsored system that is often the very aggressor against one's own clients. These are the kinds of conditions that stand at the center of a feminist of color critique of the law, a critique that does not wait for the appearance of a racial and gendered subject who is properly victimized but rather seeks to understand how gender- and sex-normative logics already drive the letter of the law, its historical legacies, and its contemporary institutions. As PJ suggests, what would it mean to focus not on the unveiling of the quivering figure but rather on how and why Asian immigrant women are positioned in need before the law to begin with? My interest is in examining how an immigration-related need—such as the need for legal status—ends up becoming part of the political project of racialized protection and punishment.

Book Description

This book is a legal ethnography of protections that unfold racial punishment to purportedly rescue immigrant women. The stories throughout analyze the legal and political conditions of Asian American advocates who attempt to access provisions provided under the Violence Against Women Act (VAWA) for their clients.[14] When VAWA was first legislated in 1994, it included a number of provisions designed to address the needs of immigrant survivors but only those who already had legal status through channels legitimized by the state (i.e., those married to citizens and their children or family members).[15] This book is primarily interested in provisions for noncitizen survivors, developed as part of reauthorizations (approximately every five years) of VAWA, the Victims of Trafficking and Violence Protection Act (VTVPA), and the Battered Immigrant Women Protection Act (BIWPA) of 2000. Namely, the U and T legal status (often referred to as "visas") that provided temporary legal status for survivors—if they agreed to prove their will and credibility to cooperate and serve the needs of police and become certified by a law enforcement or immigration official. The cooperation requirement is required via certification for the U status and included differently for T status. And this cooperation component did not go uncontested: When it was first introduced, antiviolence advocates who testified before Congress questioned the cooperation requirement, highlighting the potential harm and trauma that requiring women to work with law enforcement would cause. Congressional members emphasized instead the need for an assurance that survivors would not fall back into "cycles of violence" and justified the creation of a certification of cooperation as that assurance. Thus, we might consider that the U and T's actual design is meant for those whom the state identifies as having a specific purpose. This is deeply troubling if that purpose is to improve the longevity of policing as the only way to temporarily survive.

This book focuses on these protections and the legal requirement to cooperate. But this book is not a legal studies project; in many ways, the book strives to find ways to talk about the law without talking *like* the law. Anchored in ethnic studies and gender studies, the book theorizes the racial assemblage underpinning the victim as a legal subject used to unfurl policing. My aim is to contribute a discussion on immigration to existing abolition feminist critiques of criminalization under VAWA. Some advocates saw no future for their work unattached to police and immigration enforcement, whereas others viewed their advocacy work as navigating between the politics of antiviolence and immigrant rights, and others saw it as distinctly feminist and abolitionist. This book draws on their interpretations of the reach of law and also serves as a response to them as well. How do we understand and write about such conditions for Asian American communities and others without reifying the very terms of law itself? The chapters throughout attempt to do so by tracing categories of the human that engender the legal subject position of victim, interrogating its racial figures, and tracing how the law graphs, or writes, legal fictions. The production of this legal phenomenon renders survivors as worthy or unworthy not of mere protection but of enlistment into cooperation with police in exchange for protection.

I argue that the "undocumented crime victim" is not a person but rather a legal subject. As this book argues, VAWA's design establishes not only expectations of worthiness for protection but also qualifications to be worthy for cooperation with law enforcement as well. The law narrates this legal scheme as a *mutual exchange*, and I argue that this requirement to cooperate makes evident that the visa scheme is a law enforcement tool *first*, above any of the varied needs immigrant women may have due to their legal status or conditions of gender and sexual violence. The chapters throughout interrogate the undocumented crime victim through which survivors must match up their experiences to the racial figures of the "cooperator" with police or the "modern-day slave" but never as a someone who is part of communities experiencing state violence. Thus, the violence of legal protection, as I examine, is less defined by the absent representation of survivor voices or experiences and more evident in moments when survivors are forced to match-up their experiences to the figures the law demands.

What has this meant for our understanding of legal protection and Asian American politics around policing? Asian communities are not targeted by VAWA, nor do Asian survivors make up the majority of the applicants for U or T visas; statistically, there is no significance. Regardless of whether an argument can be made for undercounting, underreporting, or disaggregating, we can adopt a different orientation that does not rely on the logic of critical mass to justify why gender and sexual violence is relevant to contemporary Asian American politics. Or why policing is relevant as well. In similar ways, the racial assemblage of how laws and policies constitute what counts as a crime and who ought to be a criminal operates through the discursive policing of Blackness, which then has racial effects that can reorder other bodies, peoples, places, and communities. Ruth Wilson Gilmore has written that we must refuse perilous routes that attempt to search for "degrees of innocence" to rationalize who should or should not be in prisons because "there are people, inevitably, who will become permanently not innocent, no matter what they do or say."[16] In critiquing VAWA's funding of expansive policing, Mari Matsuda has written that "patriarchy has governed our thinking about crime" by instilling "its favorites" in the punishment of Blackness.[17] Anthony Farley argues that law is like a training, that it trains a continuing desire for Black criminality.[18] Writing on anti-Blackness, Sarah Haley notes that the carceral forms through the presumption that Black reproduction "breeds criminals."[19] Romina Garcia has emphasized anti-Blackness as the gratuitous violence of Black illegibility within existing anti-violence political strands that shy away from critiquing punishment.[20] I read the racial assemblage of the bind between protection and punishment to be a form of anti-Blackness particular to VAWA's broader orientation. My hope is to start from the position that VAWA's safety cannot escape its anti-Black form within modern American law because it relies on policing, and policing is structured through the systemic criminalization of Black people. For me, anti-Blackness is not the end point but rather the starting position from which I make a distinction, and simultaneously a connection, to eventually land on my critique of VAWA. While policing relies on the criminalization of Blackness, the racial assemblage of safety via legal protection continually includes and universalizes the victim as a legal subject, a policing subject that must deny its bind to a policed object. I draw this distinction so as not to sidestep the singular dynamic of anti-Blackness or conflate the racial structures of prisons with those of immigration detention, for example.

At its core, this book aims to critique the legal terms of the "victim" as belonging completely to the "criminal" subject in VAWA's pro-policing agendas (and to eventually theorize the abolition of the victim-bind). Whereas mainstream antiviolence politics have sought to humanize the victim by calling for its unsilencing, the policies that result from such politics have only resulted in reproducing universal notions of the victim. Further, only the normative subject of whiteness untouched by state-sanctioned violence can be successful in such universalisms. But as this book argues, if legal protections for survivors are bound to policing mechanisms, the universalism of the victim subject remains race and gender neutral toward criminalization lodged within the corpus of white humanity. Worse still, even a critique of such laws as dehumanizing toward communities of color still relies on the crime victim to depict and define the survivor as an excluded body opposite the human. I suggest instead that the victim is not the silenced or invisible subject opposite the human but rather that the victim is a category of the Human in Western thought, which establishes hierarchies of differentiated humanness, enforced by modern American law. Jodi Melamed and Chandan Reddy have written that categories and terms existing within contemporary politics "constitute the means of racializing human beings in order to differentially (de)value them, as necessary for existent and emergent modes of capitalist accumulation."[21] Thus, the violence I attend to is not the exclusion of Asian survivors from becoming fully realized as victims; to be clear, the violence I take issue with is the legal condition that demands that in order for a temporary form of survival to exist, one must match their interiority, their will, or what we perceive to be their empirical experience up to the expectations of what a worthy cooperator in policing should express.

Cheryl Harris has written that law is a set of expectations.[22] Not a set of rules, regulations, or hidden morals but a set of expectations tied to the objects of propertied interests. I hope to show that laws that become categorically legible as protections work through the expectation of value, that immigrants must exchange something to even come before the law, let alone receive protection. I argue that this "mutual" exchange between the state and survivors establishes a legal fiction. In a way intrinsic to its design, VAWA produces the undocumented crime victim as a figure that expands policing through the cooperation, willingness, and victimhood of survivors.

While many may caution us against critiquing the U and T visas because they are a practical tool during times of heightened anti-immigrant politics, I ask, what is so practical about turning survivors into cooperators? It has become all too acceptable to expect that immigrant communities must give something up to survive. Much of this book is a struggle to identify moments when the law fails but also when, and at whose expense, law has succeeded as a solution.

Criminalized Survivors

Over twenty-three states have mandatory arrest laws where any domestic violence call to police must result in an arrest.[23] The emphasis on arrest rather than other practices or resources has led to widely known incidents in which survivors become the ones who are arrested in order for police to fulfill a mandate.[24] Survivors acting in self-defense face increased chances of prosecution and incarceration. Existing laws impose lengthy sentences and do little to reduce violence, address racial and gendered disparities among those policed and incarcerated, or establish resources for communities.[25] Thus, advocacy efforts in some states have sought legislation for sentence reductions for survivors of domestic violence, rape, and other forms of gender-based violence who were criminalized while trying to defend or establish safety for themselves or family members in the face of abuse and harm.[26] California's prison system and police institutions continue to expand and promise public safety, but they have only resulted in the continual criminalization of Blackness to underwrite policing ideologies and narratives of support for immigration enforcement. Currently, it is much more likely to find federal funding designated to address "violence against women" distributed to police stations than to women's shelters or community resources driven by the work of people from those communities. It is no wonder, that no community has experienced an end to rape, domestic violence, or sexual assault. An organizing collective, Survived and Punished, has shown how prosecutors and parole boards consistently impose harsher sentences on survivors who act in self-defense and become targeted by law as *criminalized survivors*.[27] Alisa Bierria and Colby Lenz have argued that "failure to protect" laws, originally designed to address child neglect or abuse, are instead widely utilized by prosecutors to punish survivors acting in self-defense against abusers in domestic spaces.[28] The impact has overwhelmingly punished survivors of domestic violence and mothers.

Mimi Kim has argued that the reach of carceral logics is wide and manifests in a "fetishization of safety" within forms of community organizing and advocacy work that are otherwise critical of policing yet nonetheless find themselves facing what Kim calls the "carceral creep" within collective political formations.[29] A central division formed between those who embraced and those who refused police, and this division today remains one of the most central tensions among legal, social work, and community practices addressing gender-based violence.[30] Even further, white-dominated "violence against women" groups often maintain this division by suppressing abolitionist insights of women of color feminists who focus on the problems of state police and immigration agencies.[31] Beth Richie has argued that early antiviolence work achieved policy wins, but in the wake of these wins, the social movements of those most vulnerable were lost. Richie's framework repositions the trajectory of antiviolence law and policy as part of the historical building of a "prison nation" where the punishment of survivors and communities of color is a direct result of state divestment from the welfare, health and well-being, housing, and life-affirming needs of Black women and girls.[32] Black survivors are never quite rescued or saved as "victims" yet are often waged as spectacles to represent extremities of violence. Alisa Bierria has argued that Black survivors are vanished by certain kinds of social authoring often for the benefit of establishing the visibility of police-driven public safety narratives.[33] Thus, to even be recognized as a proper victim is to be in a position that is purely rescuable, not culpable, and thus largely distanced from symptoms of state institutions that are simultaneously humanitarian and punishing; this is a form of state violence.[34] What becomes lost is what Soniya Munshi has called the "multiplicities of violence"—structural, interpersonal, signified, and proliferated—which constitute the conditions immigrant communities of color face.[35]

Contrary to public perception, survivors do not turn immediately to law enforcement after experiencing harm, or ever.[36] While local police agencies are often quick to blame a lack of reporting on a survivor's individualized fear of the system, this ignores the institutional and accumulating harm immigrants and communities of color already face at the hands of everyday local policing, federal immigration enforcement, and collaborations between the two.[37] Andrea Ritchie has shown that for most immigrant communities, policing practices are the dominant force through which people first encounter state institutions of punishment against their legal status, gender, race, or sexuality.[38] Jonathan Simon has argued that American institutions of government utilized a specific mythologized fear of widespread crime to implement an acceptance of governance at the everyday level. Marie Gottschalk shows that even national political debates over what counts as a crime and who counts as a criminal are often the first driving force preempting broader social and economic policy agendas.[39] Further, the social history or developmental history of crime is intertwined with the racial logic of criminalization that targets Blackness, or rather, as Alisa Bierria has argued, produces a social conflation of Blackness with criminality.[40] Thus, a politics against the central criminalization of Blackness in policing is not a distraction from the problems of immigration enforcement, but rather leads to substantive critiques against immigration law and immigration agencies that manage enforcement against noncitizen communities. Currently, law enforcement agencies have produced narrative devices that state that no one should fear calling the police, yet immigrants and those most vulnerable are more often expected to call the cops and, even further, are blamed for threats to public safety when they do not do so.

VAWA, Policing, and Immigration Restrictions

Originally enacted as Title IV of the 1994 omnibus crime bill (Violent Crime Control and Law Enforcement Act), VAWA is a comprehensive federal statute to address violence against women that has since been reauthorized under the Trafficking Victims Protection Act and other appropriations statutes.[41] The main focus areas of VAWA include domestic violence, sexual assault, dating violence, stalking, campus-based violence, and sex trafficking. It is also worth noting that the vast majority of federal funding authorized through VAWA emphasizes these goals through federal grants for law enforcement or partnerships with state and nonprofit organizations.[42] For example, the largest appropriation and programmatic funding category is designated for STOP (Services, Training, Officers, and Prosecutors) grants administered under the Office on Violence Against Women.[43] This grant program is primarily designed to improve the effectiveness of law enforcement and prosecution strategies "toward violent criminal activity" and to enhance services for "victims of violent criminal activity" against women. States, US territories, and Washington, DC, are eligible for STOP grants and must allocate 25 percent to law enforcement; 25 percent to prosecutors; 30 percent to victim services (of which only 10 percent of funding within this category can be allocated to community based organizations); 5 percent to state and local courts; and 15 percent to discretionary spending.[44] In 1994, the Violent Crime Control and Law Enforcement Act (VCCLEA) distributed federal funds to states to rehire police who had been laid off and created over a hundred thousand new officer positions, allocated over one-third more funding to prisons than to preventive social and rehabilitative programs, and created the Office on Violence Against Women and the Office of Community Oriented Policing Services (COPS). Public partnerships with community policing were a priority for federal funds newly distributed to state and local governments, tribal governments, private and public entities, and multijurisdictional regions. The primary purpose was to increase the presence of policing via *cooperation* between law enforcement and community members.[45]

Both VAWA and the VCCLEA are anchored in the 1990s neoliberal ideologies and policy reforms which created particular institutional ties between punishment and social welfare. Congress passed the Personal Responsibility and Work Opportunity Reconciliation Act (PRWORA) as part of President Bill Clinton's neoliberal "make work pay" program in 1996; instead of building an accessible welfare system for food, shelter, health, and social needs, PRWORA required welfare recipients to work a minimum number of hours to be eligible to continue to receive benefits for basic needs.[46] This moment of welfare reform ended the first federal welfare program, established by the Social Security Act of 1935 and in force for sixty years, and established in its place Temporary Assistance to Needy Families (TANF), which distributed limited one-time federal block grants to states, which then determined how funds were distributed and whether state funds would supplement additional areas of need. Kaaryn Gustafson shows that rather than viewing the welfare system and law enforcement agencies as separate, the neoliberal reform established by PRWORA created structures of a new welfare system to embark on law enforcement practices of policing and criminalization against welfare recipients.[47] Dorothy Roberts's work documents a history of social workers entrenched as agents of this reform in deeply racialized and gendered ways that not only set heavier expectations on Black communities but established coercive conditions where those in poverty had to navigate a gendered welfare system that criminalized and policed their bodies and relations.[48] For example, shifting economic policies relied on neoliberal ideologies which argued that those who were poor were somehow responsible for their own poverty. These narrative ideologies often blamed the figure of Black women for "cultures of poverty" rather than the dire social policy changes that had begun to impact the entire nation. The law shifted the focus of welfare away from poverty relief, cash assistance, and benefits aimed to meet basic needs of subsistence toward policy implementations that divided the "deserving" from the "undeserving," measured by an individual's success at "responsibility" tied to work, normative performances of sexuality and social reproduction, and worthiness tied to the heteronormative family unit.

Under PRWORA, states had the option to implement lifetime bans on access for welfare benefits for anyone convicted of a drug felony. Several states still uphold this ban. Prior records, parole or probation terms, and warrants for arrest could be used by law enforcement to prohibit access not only to TANF but also to food stamps, social security, and housing. In addition, exchange of information between law enforcement and social services was enacted and aided in arrests. None of these law enforcement openings was primarily designed to aid or provide need-based assistance but rather to extend the reach of criminalization against poor communities of color. Racialized man-in-the-house rules targeted single mothers for the company they kept in their homes, family cap limits, biometric data collection, penalties for stating incorrect information on welfare documents (leading to "three-strikes-and-you're-out" outcomes), and many other administrative regulations developed from PRWORA and continue today in varying forms.[49] While welfare, immigration, and law enforcement laws and policies are constantly shifting, the legacy of this era continues into our present.[50]

PRWORA divided noncitizens, immigrant, and refugee communities into exacerbated categories of "qualified" and "unqualified" categories: Many were either newly but temporarily eligible for or restricted from accessing medical and welfare benefits based on when and how they crossed borders and whether their legal status was that of a "nonimmigrant" (generally rendered temporary) or "immigrant" (generally rendered as a potential pathway toward permanency). Qualified immigrants included refugees and asylees, legal permanent residents, and those with other forms of legal status obtained through federally managed humanitarian grounds. Unqualified categories encompassed those legally marked as undocumented or unauthorized, persons with temporary protected status, or those with temporary work visas and student visas. These were the first federally imposed uniform rules restricting states from allowing undocumented communities access to federal benefits.[51] The un/qualified distinctions created by PRWORA's language emerge here as eligibility requirements, but they are also categories of policing.[52] VAWA itself is not seen as relevant to immigration law per se, but it amends the Immigration and Nationality Act to include a number of provisions for survivors who are not US citizens.[53] Far beyond the inclusion/exclusion paradigm in immigration debates, VAWA provisions occupy the category of temporary inclusion, and the contingent temporality of these conditions highlights the primary purpose and timed value that immigrants register to the state. Here, the violence of US immigration law cannot be fully understood as merely a "broken system" that needs to be fixed but as a system that is doing the task of its design. For example, Harsha Walia reframes the very concept of nation-state boundaries to be a set of border imperialisms whereby colonial anxieties within the nation-state work to enact racial imperial expansion.[54] Naomi Paik has argued that immigration restrictions are endemic to the nation-state forms which include policing and prisons.[55] Thus, Eithne Luibhéid and Karma Chávez show how ongoing removals, detention, and criminalization rely upon the categorization of gender and sexuality via the legal status of bodies.[56] US immigration law at its lowest and highest moments of restriction also holds within its history what Hiroshi Motomura has theorized as undocumented or unauthorized persons marked as already "outside the law" while simultaneously living under law's administration and organization via education and welfare institutions, through both access and restriction, benefits and exclusions.[57]

In 1996, Congress also legislated the Antiterrorism and Effective Death Penalty Act (AEDPA) and the Illegal Immigration Reform and Immigrant Responsibility Act (IIRIRA).[58] Leisy Abrego et al., have argued that AEDPA and IIRIRA together mark a distinct moment of legal violence while also part of a longer legacy of federal agency enforcement beginning in the 1980s that criminalizes immigration. IIRIRA expanded the ability of the state to criminalize noncitizens by recategorizing misdemeanors and minor offenses into "aggravated felony" charges, restricted due process and other legal avenues by which individuals could advocate or challenge their cases, and increased federal enforcement of movement across borders through new partnerships between federal immigration agencies and local law enforcement that would increase policing contact with noncitizens.[59] The act's infamous 287(g) program, and later Secure Communities program, authorized state and local law enforcement to enter agreements with federal agencies. The primary purpose of these agreements was to form partnerships that would allow for nonfederal agencies to participate in the enforcement of federal immigration law. Local agencies could question a person about their immigration status during an arrest or at other moments when immigrants came in contact with law enforcement, arrest a person for an immigration violation, and detain persons for federal immigration agencies. The act increased federal spending for immigration enforcement and raised the required financial level for US citizens and legal permanent residents who wanted to sponsor immigrants to the United States, thereby restricting the number of potential sponsors. Most central, IIRIRA created and expanded removal proceedings to determine whether persons could remain within the nation-state. Refugee communities were suddenly impacted by IIRIRA's creation of new categories of deportation and mandatory immigration detention triggered by minor offenses and were deported to countries they had not been in for decades. The law created an expansive list of violations that would trigger removal proceedings, such as "moral turpitude," prostitution, substance-related violations, use of firearms, fleeing an immigration checkpoint, and "aggravated felonies," which triggered faster removal and detention and banned migrants from ever returning to the country.[60] The enforcement of IIRIRA made it more difficult for potential migrants to go through the process of asylum, required mandatory detention of anyone deemed subject to removal, and targeted immigration documentation and paperwork as new forms of criminality. The above is merely a short summary of the law and policy agendas that tied welfare and rescue programs (such as saving women from violence) to policing, prisons, and immigration enforcement. With this early political context in mind, this book aims to highlight the violence of legal protection when tethered to that of punishment.

Angélica Cházaro argues that immigration law produces the category of the "criminal alien" to determine eligibility, grounds for removal and so forth. Cházaro warns that immigration reform runs the risk of reproducing this very same "criminal alien" paradigm when logics of criminalization are used to determine who is removeable over others.[61] Leisy Abrego has further argued that even if someone is lawfully present with temporary legal status and allowed to remain within the nation-state, the inclusion is beholden to continued surveillance and management of those outside citizenship. The condition of legal liminality, as Jennifer Chacón has argued, produces liminal legal *subjects* who face challenges not because of the absence of rights but because of ongoing administrative management and exposure to criminal enforcement.[62] Thus, to truly critique the punishment of immigrant communities, Martha Escobar calls for abolition frameworks as the necessary path that can build political power and community formations without reproducing assimilationist agendas that justify the nonremoval of some and not all.[63] Escobar further emphasizes that the prison industrial complex is central but should not be conflated with US immigration agencies.[64]

The AEDPA expanded the monitoring of immigrant communities under counter-terrorism narratives by restricting habeas corpus relief. The statute rolled back US international human rights commitments by limiting a person's ability to challenge the terms of their detention, widening the prosecution of individuals residing within the US for actions committed outside US borders, expanding state power to categorize nongovernmental organizations or countries as terrorist groups and thus producing sanctions against them, and establishing cooperative partnerships between nation-states toward prosecution and criminalization. Rana Jaleel further highlights that rape and sexual violence become violations of international law and human rights agendas in the 1990s, tied to Cold War negotiations that entangle the recognition of sexual violence with militarized humanitarianisms and global security agendas, colonialism, and genocide.[65] Heightened racial surveillance and Islamophobia were entrenched through new national security laws and policies that racially profiled S.W.A.N.A. communities through alien registration programs, stop-and-frisk practices, border crossing and travel regulations, to name just a few.[66] These counter-terrorism agendas also promoted old tropes of women as victims of their own culture and threats to global international security regimes, religious order, and Western imperialism/humanitarianism. Thus, Nadine Naber has argued that anti-imperial approaches are necessary within women of color feminist politics that engages these ongoing surveillance practices in order to address how humanitarianism and imperialism function together to maintain and reproduce universalist narratives that seemingly allow for the recognition of violence yet mask gendered orientalist propositions. And vice versa, feminist and queer of color politics on culture must be central to any anti-orientalist framework or effort to critique the universal.[67] Particularly because state recognition of "culture" maintains universalisms even if material changes are established. For example, the relevance of culture, positioned as antithetical to the universal, can never materially or discursively emerge as a discrete whole outside universalisms in legal meaning making. That is, when culture emerges within law, for example, it is not a moment of the law's appreciation of a community's culture. Rather, Leti Volpp has shown that courts have selectively *invoked* culture to satisfy an explanation of immigrant behavior, whereas culture is rarely invoked to explain the actions of American citizen-subjects.[68] Thus, the law maintains a division between rational non-marked behaviors against the "bad behavior" of Others that require cultural explanations of the legal subject. These logics of orientalism in immigration debates emerge often through the "simple logic" that Sherene Razack has argued frames immigrants as a constant and unchanging threat to any nation-state.[69]

As this book argues, the site of safety and rescue highlights the need not only to continue the critique of criminalization and immigration enforcement but to do so without reifying the sexualized, gendered, and racial logics of victimhood that become naturalized by the legal subject position of the victim in law. Thus, a critical approach to VAWA shifts and opens up existing scholarship on violence against women but also contributes to interventions within scholarship on immigration law and borders.

Methodology: Abolition Feminisms, Feminist Refusals, and Legal Ethnography

Angela Davis, Gina Dent, Erica Meiners, and Beth Richie write that abolition feminism is a relationality; they trace the relations in theory and thought that formed between and simultaneously through feminist antiviolence movements which critique safety and protection and abolition movements to end punishment and prisons. An abolition feminist lens, for them, emphasizes the work of "reframing the terrain" on which struggle takes place.[70] If we are to think through the conditions immigrant survivors face, this requires the reframing of the terrain to include a critique of protection and to expand the terrain of Asian immigrant rights agendas to take gender and sexual violence as central to analyses and political formations. Alisa Bierria, Jakeya Caruthers, and Brooke Lober emphasize that abolition feminism is not so much about an orientation toward the end resolution but rather about abolishing that which is "so deeply rooted that it disciplines meaning itself."[71]

Much of the ethnographic writing in this book refuses protection as legal meaning making in order to retell a path to abolish the victim within our politics and to unsettle how the legal subject of the victim shapes how we relate to others and is consistently sanctioned by the state. I discuss abolition feminisms as a practice and orientation that imagines futurities without the normalization and naturalization of punishment: not a correction or improvement of punishment but a commitment to the unknown and yet-to-be-articulated possibilities. Abolition feminisms also theorize violence in a particular way, where the political, personal, or collective goal is often not focused on eradicating violent subjects from society but, rather, on knowing what it means to live with violence so that we can creatively and accountably live otherwise. I do not engage abolition feminisms as a theory that can lend itself to more particular ethnic empiricisms; rather, intersecting movements of antiprison, anticarceral, decolonial, transnational, queer and trans of color, disability justice, and feminist antiviolence movements allow us to see how structures and institutions are violent when they continually reinforce racial hierarchies among us in order to protect and rescue us. If a feminist and queer politics relies on punishment or if an anticarceral or antiprison position sidesteps protection, neither contends with the racial critique of abolition feminisms.

I understand abolition feminist thought to have never been without its epistemological roots in Black feminisms as they engage with movements to address gender-based violence and prison abolition. My concern is not so much around pairing abolition feminisms with Asian American feminisms or creating an ethnically specific abolition feminism. To be clear, I am not arguing that one's specific histories or communities are not pertinent to notions of the self. But I am saying that even before we do anything with lived experience, we must grapple with the fact that there is a level of violence that occurs when the only way one can speak before the law is to match experience to the expectations of a legal figure that already precedes.[72] Often protection falls under the radar of critiques of the violence of immigration. However, abolition feminist theorizations relentlessly remind us that we do not protect each other; we care for each other. The law protects, and we do not; the law cannot escape its own interiority of punishment, but we can build otherwise. This line of thinking unbinds protection from care, law from relationality, and does so without blame or shame for those who still work with or have little choice but to utilize law even while experiencing punishment by state agencies.

For me, an abolition feminist critique *of law* starts with the solution itself, in particular, political discourses that rely on an acceptance of punishment and the promise of public safety that places demands upon the vulnerability of those with the least resources to act properly, cooperate, and improve safety for everyone else. I refer to "cooperation" as a legal fiction.[73] For me, legal fiction is a genre of law's writing to establish definitive rules and regulations that produce violence, but not because of any error or misrepresentation between lived experience and law; rather, in this genre of law, racial figures are constantly produced by fixed legal subject positions on which the maintenance of the legal bind between protection and punishment is dependent. Violence occurs when experiences are only legible as a universal and racially neutral figure attached to an object in order to either disprove unworthiness or demonstrate worthiness to qualify for a legal benefit. For example, the figure of the "cooperator" attached to the improvement or benefit of policing shades and controls the limits through which survivors can enter the legal subject position of the crime victim. Without reconceptualizing the "mutual exchange" between police and survivors as a legal fiction, the bind between protection and punishment is completely and tragically normalized.

Several refusals orient the theories, ethnography, and writing practices that make this book. The first is a refusal of survival narratives as a *precursor* to the violence of law. While dominant women's rights campaigns repeatedly call for the unsilencing of rape victims, this particular set of politics results primarily in efforts to gain more recognition from the law and ultimately the state. As such, the kinds of voices that can be successfully transitioned from being silenced to unsilenced are often those that provide spectacular evidence, the most damaged experience, and the most rescued possibility. This latter point is the most vivid anchor of the book's focus on legal protection as an exchange that produces racial violence and exacerbates the policing of gender. Indeed, an arsenal of feminist decolonial and anti-imperial works have argued that the very telling and viewing of sexual violence is already part of the broader gendered structures of the Western gaze, homonormative political campaigns, humanitarian morality policing, colonial savior distortions, and the very impossibility of sexual violation against the not quite human. My focus is on how the law desires these voices insofar as they provide stories of experience that match up to racial figures produced by the letter of the law. The concern is less with a critique of authenticity and more with the function of violent experiences as the prerequisite stronghold for any writing on law and gender-based violence. As a refusal practice focused on law, the book strives to work through gender violence without reinforcement from survivors' voices as evidence. To be clear, I am in no way arguing against the power of voice or survivor narratives. I am instead attempting to interrogate beyond experiences that are vividly violent and toward a different site of law—where the making of a legal subject must match up to a racial figure.

Laura Kang has argued that the "Asian/American" woman is a troubling subject when configurations and interpretations of image, identity, and subjectivity do not line up with each other. Here Kang asks, How is the discernment of Asian American women made through the nonequivalence of the Asian and American body? Further, Kang writes, "If there must be a field of study called 'Asian American women's history,' it must work *through* scrutinizing—and not compensating—for the particular limits of the archives and their possible (re)-narrations as tangled up with the hierarchical particularization of national bodies and subjects."[74] From here, the unsilencing of a particular ethnic voice (either in singularity or in its liberal twin, allyship) continues to hold experience captive to the existing archived terms of law if inclusion and incorporation are not interrogated. My ethnographic writing throughout this book is less about victim experiences and more about violences of nuanced convergence between the letter of the law and advocacy practice, and, the political tensions between immigration rights, antiviolence, and abolition orientations within and across Asian American contemporary political movements. I chose to conduct an ethnography of law's writing and the graphing of legal rules and regulations that become interpreted, articulated, and translated by the practitioners who attempt to use them. And in my fieldwork I observed that *protections* incorporated, and even desired, women's stories—but primarily those restrictively bound to punishment. Because of this, the project's refusal to rely on victimization as a precursor is not so much a rejection of experience or denial of violence but a refusal of what Joan Scott has called "the evidence of experience."[75] When excavations of experience stand in for race in the law, this approach runs the risk of reinforcing legal records rather than challenging them.

Eve Darian-Smith has argued that legal ethnographies as a genre shift from exploring the causal effects of the technical or institutional site of law toward an orientation of the legal and social subject.[76] The writing of narrative, relations of power, personal and social response, and historical formation "against culture," rather than its essentialism, gives way to legal phenomena of different scholarly forms extending outside and beyond the letter, formal legal actors, or the case record.[77] Susan Coutin and Barbara Yngvesson argue that law neither discovers nor invents social realities. Instead, legal ethnographies emerge through multiple locations and temporalities, where even the "field" from which data are collected shifts due to ethnographic practices that in effect materialize around the ethnographer.[78] The critique of positivist empiricism in law should also include an analysis of race. Thus, I understand critical race theory to be a body of literature which argues that race and racism are endemic to law rather than external to it. Writing against critical legal theorists who render race to be tangential to law, critical race theory argues instead that race and racism are not only evident in but entirely inherent to the foundations of American law in rights, liberties, property, and personhood.

Further, Denise Ferreira da Silva highlights that critical race theory's particular formulation relies heavily on the exclusion of racial differentiation from law as the basis for critique. If the rights-bearing subject (as the primary subject) must first be excluded from law, and if that exclusion can be legible only through one's racial differentiation, then this line of critical race theory runs the same "socio-logical" liberal rendering of race in absentia.[79] Ferreira da Silva argues instead that the racial (and not race differentiation) produces the domain of universality (law) rather than only making such universalisms evident when excluded by the presence of a racial body. In my view, the relationship of experience to the victim as a legal subject is particularly relevant to this debate. For Sora Han, the foundation of modern American law rests in what she formulates as the fantasy of color blindness in law's writing (i.e., judicial opinions) which establishes authority through an arrangement of past and future. Thus, Han writes that there is an "originary limit" of modern American law that legal practices must always *write*: "The fantasy of colorblindness, as an iterative form of physical foreclosure imposed on the legal text works against this plural temporality, and holds out a more manageable diagnostic understanding of the history of legal reform, whether episodic, cyclical, or progressive."[80] For the study of race and law, then, Han puts forward a framework where the examination of race is not so easily resolved at the site of the material condition, nor is it wholly apparent as a critique of social effects, racism of the past, or prescribed impacts. Rather, a critical theorization of race must attend to what Han calls the "poetics of the plea," which ultimately attends to law's language, reads engagement with law as an inventive practice and political struggle, and brings forward the site of law as a practice of writing. This path is paramount, and I draw heavily from this approach. I have noted throughout that anti-Blackness is a central framework that makes possible a critique of the *policing* function of visa provisions, which are not traceable on the surface of VAWA law as a protection. And thus the racial bind between policing (punishment) and visas (protection) cannot be easily found in bodily evidence or the material application of law's letter because VAWA laws are designed in the reverse.

From the beginning, I never sought to record the stories of survivors. Rather, I hoped to show that a study of gender violence and law had a place without relying on the voice of survivors or stories of violence, trauma, or harm. Because I saw how the law constantly desired representations of damage and depletion of a very gendered kind, I attempted to practice a refusal of this proposed necessity. My attempts were filled with difficulty along every moment of this path, but this difficulty was never about the challenges of ethically representing what advocates said or accurately depicting the scenarios they were in. Rather, I was confronted with what it meant to ethnographically participate with someone while having disagreements about the law, to write about the harms of a law while also being a part of social movements and organizing efforts to support those who partially benefited from such laws, and to think through what someone else is saying without losing or betraying what you yourself are saying. Advocacy services are perhaps self-evidently not poetic; they are rarely thought of in such a way. But paying attention to the *graphing* of legal ethnography became the only way I was able to theorize race, gender, and the violence of law through law's writing and the way we write about the law.

Legal ethnography, as I conduct it, focuses on impasses between letter and practice—by tracing how the law writes racial figures to establish the constant limit of legal protection. Initially, my research began with a set of questions about whether immigrant women were truly being protected by the law, what the law was doing to survivors, and whether it could be changed. But as advocates began to share their interpretations and stories with me, there was often a slight break, an awkwardness, between words they chose as their own and those they simply had to repeat because there were no other words provided by law—*victim, criminal, perpetrator, unauthorized*. It was impossible for them to talk about the work of advocacy without constant qualifiers before and after certain repeating terms. Struggles such as these shape much of the theorization surrounding the approach to ethnographic story not only in terms of my approach to what was spoken but also in terms of the very location of words in legal practices and the letter of the law.

The advocates I interviewed often shared interpretations and insights about certification requirements as they walked me through the step-by-step process. The descriptions included stories about law as not merely a rule that stands on its own but a set of expectations that shaped how one could actually advocate for a client, the struggle of having to assist a client in presenting their interiority or willingness in tangible material terms despite the intangible and immaterial subject position that the law had already demanded. Their stories raised another question: What makes someone free from legal status? Expectations of interiority are another site of legal violence through which undocumented immigrant women are shuttled between innocence and culpability. Advocacy work for survivors entails not only adjustments around legal status but mental health and health services, housing needs, childcare, work authorization, transportation, cash assistance, wellness—and countless other areas of immediate assistance.

During my fieldwork I conducted weekly participant observation and semistructured interviews and follow-up visits with nonprofit staff in the San Francisco Bay Area serving primarily Asian immigrant women and their families.[81] Separately, during this time and prior, I was active in local and national collective organizing spaces addressing gender and sexual violence, prison abolition, and reentry that shaped my thinking and writing. But in my ethnographic practices, I focused most of my time with an Asian American–serving law center, and from there I moved around a lot, from San Francisco, East Bay, and South Bay, to interview staff at different nonprofits all focused on serving Asian clients. I attended and helped organize community events, some of which were tied directly to legal advocacy work and others of which were focused on feminist of color abolitionist and antiprison efforts. Because the organization's legal work encompassed partnerships with social service agencies, women's shelters, and community services, I often engaged with case managers and staff from other organizations. Unlike in most ethnographic studies, the practice of legal protection is less able to fit the model of a discrete nonprofit organization or state institution but rather encompasses a shifting set of efforts centered on a stage of legal phenomena across multiple institutions of state violence.

When I first worked with a domestic violence organization in San Francisco, I learned about the new U and T visas and how advocates understood them and anticipated their possibilities. I returned a year later to more fully research the unfolding of the U and T visas for this book. I spent one year, and then another, volunteering with an Asian American–serving legal center while attending events and programs and interviewing community programming staff and attorneys at the organization, as well as caseworkers and attorneys across ten other organizations in San Francisco, East Bay, and the South Bay. I conducted weekly participant observation over a two-year period, conducted two rounds of thirty-two semistructured interviews, attended events and workshops, databased cases, assisted with office tasks, and helped with fundraising events. This book's ethnographic writing follows shifting laws while also attempting to anchor analysis in the clustering of Asian American advocacy efforts, which also constantly moved. The advocates I interviewed and observed came from a range of client services; some had begun their work only a year earlier, and others had been with their organization for over a decade. As is common with nonprofit work in the United States, there is high turnaround and almost all of the advocates I spoke with now work at different organizations or in completely different areas of employment. Thus, the temporal conditions of advocacy work varied greatly, as did their sociopolitical constructions.

The term *advocate* in this book refers to a wide range of people based on their engagements with legal institutions and laws. I have chosen to write with the word *survivor* throughout. However, the law's own terms will always refer to immigrant or undocumented survivors as a *crime victim* as this is the legal subject position in which one must stand to access VAWA, and it will use *noncitizen* or *foreign national*, as defined legally, to refer to those who are not US citizens and are thus the target of the provisions I focus on. The chapters throughout aim to raise the supposed seamlessness, the ease, and the legal moments of "matching" by tracing the legal fictions of VAWA's design and the racial figures that presuppose it. Nothing in this book can fully resolve the tension between the words *survivor* and *victim*, nor is any aspect of this book focused on this resolution. Rather, I write with *survivor* to signify a feminist refusal of victimhood and victimization as descriptors of migrant women, on the one hand, and to allow for an opening to theorize the episteme of the victim as a legal subject, on the other. But more important, much of the work in this book shows that to write with *survivor* as a word is not to intend or aim for a substitution but rather to attempt a project of abolishing the victim as a legal enclosure.

Chapter Descriptions

Chapter 1 provides the book's theory of writing about law, the argument of ethnographic impasse, and refusal as an approach toward voice and evidence.[82] Chapter 2 focuses on racial figures tied to cooperation and mutual exchange with policing and legal protections designed to provide solutions for survivors without legal status. Chapter 3 theorizes the crime victim as a legal subject attached to the racial figure of the "modern-day slave," injury, and contractability in antitrafficking campaigns. The conclusion sets abolition feminist critiques against victimhood in conversation with contemporary pro-policing politics emerging within political reform efforts and discourses attached to the label of anti-Asian hate.

Conclusion

What, then, is legal protection, and what are its legal fictions? To be configured by the law's writing, to be legible by the making of legal meaning, and to undergo the conditions of an entire legal enterprise? To be the thing that a legal fiction identifies as its figure? Legal fiction as not fictive but a genre of law's writing, its material form, where the possibility of a subject outlines the narrative discourse of meaning and the rule of law. Or in other words, what kind of law is before us when the function of its object invents a new kind of subject that repeats the memory of its form? In the absence of any kind of body that matches up to the law's configurations, we can only, and not without difficulty, trace legal fictions that outline the figures that restrain women's lived experiences—these disciplines of the human category move migrants into the "body of the civil" and are a form of enforcement that reflects the already racial and gendered violence of law's writing. Legal protections that present themselves as solutions are perhaps always at the forefront of any critical inquiry that takes racial differentiations to be objects that give meaning to law's violence. For while the law is relentlessly redundant about who ought to be punished and what should count as crime, it is far less forthcoming about when and how it protects. And for this reason, approaches to the role of race and sexuality through which legal meaning is made have often had to theorize and create around law's fixed words. Punishment has always been a part of how immigrants, refugees, and diasporas navigate movements through US borders. However, policing, in particular, is less discussed in Asian American studies.[83] This book suggests a different orientation, one that practices a politics of refusal against the colonial logic of empirical evidentiary necessity and turns instead toward an embrace of the struggle to engage with abolition feminisms.

My work leading up to this book grapples with the insufficiencies of the ontology of the survivor, the limits of the subject whose excavated existence was supposed to correct that of the victim, and has largely done so. Yet, if to survive is to live beyond the life of others, if death must always be present for this survival, then the direction from which survival unfurls comes from the kind of violence that is never temporary and indeed promises to never be so. When law enacts and materially *enforces* investment in our survival and when that investment is determined by the longevity of the law and not the life of a person or a community, racial violence and sexual violence do not end.

1

Writing Against Legal Fictions

FEMINIST REFUSALS, THE VICTIM,
AND ETHNOGRAPHIC IMPASSE

Not everyone has a complete story, and not everyone can afford to tell the stories they might have. Because of this, writing about gender and sexual violence might always involve accountability over who holds stories and for what purposes. Survivors of violence may be the ones who know this in a specific way. With law, stories are inevitably translated in part or in full by the letter and its institutions; the experience, memory, and affect are made purposeful. On what terms does a story become successful under law? This chapter begins a series of small critiques around law's successful stories. This approach analytically opens interrogations into paradigms of white injury, as well as the legal remedies they dominate; "breaking the silence" is a political claim over stories that have been silenced. But the reasons why stories are not told are not the same as why they are not heard. And thus, for this reason, when silence refers simultaneously to the problem of not being told and the effect of not being heard, this political claim is unable to account for the gendered and racial conditions that unevenly produce why some stories are valued over others.

I am not arguing that communities of color and Indigenous activists do not also utilize this unsilence/silence political framework, but I am saying that we and others are not the ones most funded, heard, or granted power for it. Further, while I understand why breaking the silence is a political strategy, the trouble lies in the treatment of survivors only as silenced victims and never as *already speaking*. In many ways, the disavowal of the already speaking is an affective colonial formation remade through heteropatriarchal logics; it is entwined within state humanitarian rescues, salvage ethnographies, the politics of saving, and patriarchal protection. As Maile Arvin, Eve Tuck, and Angie Morrill have argued, attending to this set of conditions is at stake for any feminist discourse.[1] If the political narration casts survivors as breaking away from a period of silence, this means they already tried to speak prior. Frankly, the event that marks others as never having spoken is a white fantasy. Why does this continue to reside in some feminist political desires, and how has this desire reproduced our inabilities to interpret legal meaning in the absence of this kind of story? I want to be clear that I am in no way arguing against storytelling, against survivor stories, or against myself or others who speak. But I am pushing for a differentiation between stories we might tell and the law's writing of what Joan Scott has called the "evidence of experience."[2] In fact, much of this book uses stories, but also the legal fictions the law attempts to tell.

As a political discourse, "breaking the silence" often relies on the imagery of a particular kind of victim; one who acts, sounds, and looks like the perfect victim must be damaged but cannot ever be completely damaged, just damaged enough so that there is still the possibility for something to be successfully restored.[3] But in order to draw attention to the racial and gendered political economy of victimhood, the writings of abolitionist organizers have tirelessly shown how social services and aid within the US nonprofit industrial complex are often still caught within the logics of state enforcement and the requirements for successful behaviors. Thus, the political reach that overemphasizes silence employs a certain level of safety and comfort with the move to invite state institutions and practices into people's lives. In some ways, this safety includes a racial violence already paid by others—those who can never be allowed to stand in the origin position from which the value of restoration can be accumulated. How, then, might ethnographic writing approach the violence *of* the law while writing about violence and the law? To draw from Dina Georgis, there is at stake the ongoing relational practice of writing, telling, and listening to, and for, a *better story* that might affectively shift away from colonial bookends of resistance and emancipation as well as reveal what has already been there.[4] I have attempted to trace the grammar of the legal subject in order to interrogate how the experiences of survivors are made to match up to particular racial figures to become legally legible. My aim was to create a different set of research questions on law, without relying on the damaged voice as evidence but not letting go of stories that require retelling to critique the law.

In "Venus in Two Acts," Saidiya Hartman writes that the archive is like a death sentence; to appear in slavery's record was to appear through death and disposable objects, records, and inventories. To bring forward the violence of the Atlantic slave trade that made one's appearance in the archive quite literally a death sentence, Hartman writes that her practice was not to tell the stories of young women and girls but to write about the "resistance of the object." She writes, "And how does one tell impossible stories? Stories about girls bearing names that deface and disfigure, about the words exchanged between shipmates that never acquired any standing in the law and that failed to be recorded in the archive, about the appeals, the prayers, and secrets never uttered because no one was there to receive them."[5] I raise Hartman's words here because these impossible stories are so completely dissimilar to those presented in this book. And because of this, they urge us to pause. Hartman's move to theorize and write the resistance of the object pushes us to contend with the objects tethered to the subject in law. The difficulty she identifies urges a different orientation for writings about violence and law. That is, law produces conditions one is required to undergo in order to become a subject that carries, or carries out, the object of law's desire. The impossible stories reorient how we understand and write about those possible narratives produced through law. I am making a distinct move here, to take a cue from what we cannot ask of Black women and girls in the legal record—those impossible stories—to guide a refusal of law's attempts to reproduce the legibility of only certain figures and configured narratives. If we interrogate the stories law urges *to be possible*, we can begin to critique the legal fictions and racial figures tied to such possibilities and the violences they mask as protection, rescue, and restoration.

This chapter draws on a series of irreconcilable and dissonant moments in my ethnographic work, revealing what I call *ethnographic impasses* between me and the legal and social advocates I interviewed. Drawing on feminist theorizations of story, writing, and knowledge production, I argue that a particular practice of feminist refusals becomes necessary in order to write ethnographically without reproducing the law's own terms. My hope was this: A feminist critique of law strives to write about the law without talking like the law. I suggest a turn that pushes us to identify what we would have to refuse in order to avoid reproducing the law's terms of protection. In doing so, we can move toward abolishing protection's bind to punishment, abolishing the expectations that victimize experiences rather than liberating them, and ultimately abolishing the victim that may be within ourselves.

Writing and the Legal Graph

In the beginning, readers rarely asked why the voices of survivors were not present in my writing. I thought nothing of this at first. To me, the project itself and the political work I found myself committed to were always about Asian American women, survivors, communities, our politics, and our lives. But for many broader audiences, it is unfathomable and even egregious that research on gender-based violence and the law would not present the stories of violence. A colleague reading my work once added the word *victim* next to every sentence with the word *advocate*. This initial misreading led to a series of questions: How much, or how little, to tell, and whether to tell at all—each question is simultaneously the method by which one approaches the law, what is initially considered to be law and what is not, and how one writes. In my view, law binds things and people together by enforcement and narrates through the implementation of expectation. I turn critical attention toward the law's insistence on the bind that shapes constraints among advocacy practices and also emerges as impasses within my own ethnographic writing.

In my initial interviews, I observed advocates who worked with laws that actually desired stories, victim accounts, and voices of depletion. I saw the continued presence of certain valued stories over others that were fraught, stuck, yet repeating. Laws that are designed to protect from "violence against women" as a specific formulation establish protection that must be enforced within a specific order: to improve police first and then protect survivors. We can call this a contradiction or paradox between the subject and object of law, but the criticism reaches a limit when the law actually follows through with its promise. Particularly in the case of immigration provisions legislated through the normalization of policing in the Violence Against Women Act (VAWA), the legal subject binds protection and punishment not because the law fails to protect immigrant survivors but because the law enforces that protection and delivers it in a particular way. For here survivors are both subject and object, both the protected and those enlisted into punishment. Under this liberal arrangement of law, the state is less invested in a complete wholesale silencing or exclusion of the subject outside of citizenship. Thus, if our critiques of law's power hinge only on cases where protection is denied, then such protection is rendered as an exception, and the legal subject is also rendered as such. For even when an existing law may appear to fail survivor communities, the structure and design of this particular law can still remain—at its base level, an example of reform. The remnant pushes us to go beyond the contradiction or misrepresentation and to seek instead the assemblage that maintains the violence of law itself.

At the core of my approach is an attempt to write about the law without relying on the violence of its own terms and without reproducing or reifying its preconditions. The kind of writing I attempt to exemplify here is as much a theorization as it is a practice or a method, an analysis, and an argument. I aim toward a feminist refusal of how the law speaks, not just what its impact is on the speaking. What would it mean to write about the violence of law without the story of violence after victimhood? Or to engage a writing practice that refuses the story the law demands in order to retell the law's own writing? Linda Tuhiwai Smith has written that "research is linked in all disciplines to theory" and that "reading, writing, talking [are] all as fundamental to academic discourse as science, theories, methods, paradigms."[6] In writing on Indigenous knowledges and a critique of research methods formed by Western imperialism and colonialism, Smith has shown that who writes and how one writes are inextricably tied to the theories and paradigms that emerge from knowledge production. No academic endeavor can escape the ongoing centering of Western thought that continually builds tools of research that submerge Indigenous people (and thus Indigenous knowledge formations) and rely on the repetition of this move. The impossibility of escape extends to American law as well. We must also understand the letter of the law and legal institutions to be endemic to these forms of modernity. We might refuse law's attempts to exceptionalize gender and sexual violence and disavow the ties between legal protections and the colonial structures of modern American law.[7] In doing so, this also challenges Asian American communities to think through the stakes of who and how protection and punishment are valued and enforced.

How a nation-state protects reveals how it governs and yields control through selective saving; these are but some of the heteropatriarchal conditions of settler colonialism. Further, in my view, the colonial dyad of silence/speech reproduces itself within the victim/perpetrator legal entanglement. Here, when gender violence is understood to occur only within the interpersonal formation of a singular victim opposite a singular perpetrator, not only does this framing grossly misrepresent interpersonal violence as something to be wholly resolved at the level of the individual, but this framing also excuses systemic violences that materially and discursively produce the racial and gendered "criminal" *and* "victim." Audra Simpson writes that even within engagements between and among ethnographers and interlocutors, refusals occur in both ethnographic practice and its writing. The ethnographic refusal in Simpson's formulation is not simply a rejection of something or a cutting off but rather a turning away and a turning toward elsewhere that reveals both iterative sites of colonialism from the turning point and Indigenous critique in what is beyond the refusal (or in it).[8] The refusal thus also opens up the possibility of critique (among many existing others) against colonialism's gendering normalizations and hierarchies, which, in my reading, ground and mask sexual violence. While the text is not focused on sexual violence, I draw from Simpson's descriptor of ethnographic refusal to connect retelling as a distinct formulation away from the colonial dyad of silence/speech reproduced by the liberal politics of silence/unsilence in victim-centered mainstream antiviolence politics. Here, refusal is a simultaneous response and critique that replaces the emphasis on silence with an *awareness* of retelling what is remembered, lived, or felt.

Dian Million has written that what is experienced and what has been experienced by Indigenous peoples are registers that narrate; they are not reflective of or responsive to dominant forms, and because of this, they are often deeply threatening to nation-states. Million theorizes "felt theory" as a self-determination that presents Indigenous knowledge and Indigenous women's voices as simultaneously a critique of the ordering of colonial histories and a pathway toward new orderings.[9] Felt theory thus refuses the reconciliations of Western nation-states that take on therapeutic state treatments—which has pushed me to view legal protections differently. I raise this discussion to highlight Million's critique of American law, which she argues is both a trace and a presence of colonialism. As trace and presence, law is constantly working and maintaining rather than remembering or retelling. In my view, knowing these epistemologies inevitably challenges any writing on legal protection. Thus, it is impossible to think through how survivors experience the law without thinking through both the racial and gendered conditions of the legal subject that survivors must match up to, and critiquing what presupposes that subject at the epistemological level. This approach theorizes from a distinctly different position than those that expect the subject of feminist thought as one which must always resist to then be relevant to our writing.

A belabored example: Survivors who seek out legal remedies often cannot appear as resisting subjects in their engagement with law but rather must be victim subjects whose racial and gendered experiences are compartmentalized as they become legible figures worthy of the task of cooperation and policing. It is a domesticated and passive configuration. Even further, survivors who resist are continually criminalized for resisting; defending of the self is viewed through existing racial categories of victimhood and criminality, rooted in whiteness and criminalization of Blackness in US policing. We might consider how law's promises and solutions are iterative of violence. When those most vulnerable are made to rely on a legal promise, the practice of refusal and retelling helps us to articulate more deeply the racial assemblage of that promise, the hierarchical differences it creates, and its cost (and who bears that cost). Policy solutions that provide resources to vulnerable communities are distinctly different from those that expect these same communities to become social solutions to benefit everyone else. Further, law promotes and creates legal meaning making, often wielding the visibility of women's vulnerability and using the experiences of survivors as evidence of criminality—an already racialized and gendered political project that enacts violence on all communities to which survivors belong.

This does not render law to be a false object. While *victim* has many colloquial meanings, I am focusing here on the victim as a specific constitution of law's making—a legal phenomenon—where one becomes legally legible. Saidiya Hartman writes, "Not only was rape simply unimaginable because of purported black lasciviousness, but also its repression was essential to the displacement of white culpability that characterized both the recognition of black humanity in slave law and the designation of the black subject as the originating locus of transgression and offense."[10] When we center the Black subject in American law's specific construction of consent, we are confronted with a repeating presence of the submergence of sexual violence within the emergence of the modern legal subject of humanity. I raise this to say, if some are never recruited into or eligible for being subjects of sexual violence, the more established proper victim requires continual critique not for its privileges but for its purpose and value added to state violence.

Experience

CC: Why are you asking me these questions?

ME: [Pause] The last question?

CC: Oh no, no. I'm just wondering about the questions about law enforcement. Because our clients, Asian women, compared to, let's say, the Latino community, don't have as many problems with police.

CC asked for my response toward the tail end of our conversation as we discussed what the purpose of my research was, how I was feeling, and how she was feeling after having such a long conversation. I had asked CC a series of questions about Asian immigrant women and their experience navigating pressures to cooperate with local law enforcement, or cooperate with federal immigration agencies. When she asked, "Why are you asking me these questions?" she went on to explain her thoughts on why questions about law enforcement or cooperation with the police seem a better fit for organizations working with Latinx immigrant women. PL suggested these visas did not represent a "sea change" for the Asian American community when compared to Latinx communities. I tried to present the best response I could, which at the time consisted of no more than a jumble of thoughts about why the absence of a critical mass of Asian immigrant women was not a deterrent for me. I said I needed to think more about her question and spent the next few days wondering, "Am I asking the wrong questions?"

CC's request for my response and the vague moment between us represented an impasse, one that eventually developed into an identifiable ethnographic moment, originally ignored and then later retrieved. This was an ethnographic moment of no experience, a moment explicitly about the lack of critical mass, about the suggestion that perhaps Asian American problems were less appropriate. The possibility of developing critiques around policing and protection was almost foreclosed in CC's question and the anxiety-ridden confusion as to whether a law that does not represent a critical mass of Asian immigrants should still be part of contemporary scholarship in Asian American studies. Her very suggestion of what a non–Asian American experience might be opened up an interpretation for me, one that might set the impasse as an approach to the study of Asian Americans, race, and the law. In this way, experience is not equated with evidence, and, more important, the absence of experience is not a reification of how "other" experiences are deemed to be racial problems. This book has argued that one way that legal violence unfolds is through the regulation that survivors must match up their experiences to racial and gendered figures of policing and security in order to be eligible for legal protection. Here, this moment between CC and me provided an opening for refusal, for refusing the dimension of law's role in shaping what we perceive to be relevant to Asian immigrant experience. Asian Americans do not have to wait to be properly represented as targets of policing in order to form a politics about policing. The moment between CC and me was perhaps an orientation that might constitute an Asian American feminist insight, even in the absence of a visible speaking ethnic subject as a formal legal actor. Grace Hong has written that even Asian American feminist spaces move between multiple women of color spaces, which themselves are anchored in specific analytics and politics of difference while simultaneously drawing analyses from outside and across political communities.[11]

Sora Han asks what limits the category of Asian American jurisprudence when Asian legal actors do not exemplify an ethnically or racially particular experience. While this book is not focused on the question of jurisprudence per se, I draw from Han to theorize what Asian American Studies needs to refuse or retell, when the ethnographic informant or racial legal actor speaks through the racial logics of the law (and its legal fictions) rather than challenging it. In other words, if the study of law is only relevant when there is first a racial subject defined by its speech or as a speaking subject, the already existing racial parameters of color-blind logics are often either reinforced despite the presence of the ethnic speaking legal actor. In the antidiscrimination case Han explores, Chinese American plaintiffs articulated their racial position against Blackness in order to argue that they should receive protection like whites, not from white supremacy.[12] Not only does Han's reading suggest that the relevance of Asian identity cannot be conflated with the racial figure under the legal subject, but further, her critique also identifies the form and power of law to be a racial assemblage rather than viewing law as a neutral site through which race expresses itself. In other words, Han argues further that "racial jurisprudence is precisely the *case of the split* between the particular and the universal that law's language circles around ... concerned with the development of a capacity that illuminates the peculiarity of the particular (claimant) and the force of the universal (claim)."[13] This reminder is imperative. For example, I center my discussions of gender violence and Asian American legal advocacy on VAWA law. Yet VAWA has no traceable racial target on its surface (even eligibility is framed as gender neutral). This law is not categorized as Asian American per se, but this does not mean that there is no impact on Asian survivors or that domestic violence, rape, or sexual assault is somehow irrelevant to Asian and Asian American communities. We must challenge the concept of critical mass and the speaking legal actor *as precursors*, and in doing so, Asian American feminist theorizations can refuse the uncritical embrace of the crime victim.

The U and T visas and all VAWA provisions operate through a "color-blind" racial logic—Anyone can apply; there is no racial exclusion or gender-specific benefit. This is particularly important to grasp, because these provisions, as I have argued throughout, provide relief without racially differentiating in their legal design. I am not arguing, though, that we should let go of racial difference. Rather, I am saying the power of law is not merely evident at the site of the social that passively reflects back what law does; instead, the letter of the law is a site of racial assemblage of such things as criminalization and the entanglement of protection with policing in VAWA's form. In my work, I theorize out of this bind through a critique of the law's letter and practice that produce racial differences which resignify punishment as protection. Alexander Weheliye has theorized racial assemblages as a "set of sociopolitical processes that discipline humanity" rather than a biopolitical or cultural classification.[14] In this way, race is not additive to the human but rather endemic, and thus constitutive of humanity, political claims for humanization, categories of the human in law, and legal human rights versus humanitarianisms.[15]

Kimberlé Crenshaw's text "Mapping the Margins," on intersectionality, critical race theory, and law, begins with a discussion of domestic violence shelters and Asian survivors and the experiences of Black women caught at the margins of antiracist and antisexist politics.[16] While intersectionality is often referenced as a descriptor of multiple overlapping racial identities broadly speaking (often inviting whiteness), Crenshaw's text, as I read it, is instead quite specific and critiques the law's "single axis framework" which constraints how legal claimants can become legible under only one protected class even when the violation they face occurs because of multiple categories their lives occupy.[17] That is, appeals to the law are most successful when confined to either the logic of gender or race, but never both. Because of this limitation, Crenshaw calls for structural, political, and representational intersectionality to interrogate both law and political formations. In my reading, intersectionality as an approach to law lends itself to a theorization of the violence of certain legal remedies and binary political agendas that are inadvertently produced *for the law* versus for the survivor. Crenshaw outlines a suggestive way to read legal advocacy as a site of intersecting structures of law and its institutions as well. Further, the text gestures to the politics among women of color antiviolence advocates and the predominance of whiteness and the criminalization of Blackness. Crenshaw highlights white feminist advances to pass laws addressing rape and domestic violence in this moment and the specific need to map the epistemological boundaries of law.[18] Further, Priscilla Ocen argues that the single-axis position reinforces not just the claimant or "victim" but the law's production of "criminal," always striving to make it singularly about Blackness and in particular Black masculinity.[19]

How can we approach something like VAWA law to reveal how the racial gives meaning, how it engulfs race difference, and, last, how this strategy manipulates bodies (visa status applicants and advocates) and hierarchically arranges them into interiorities that have differing values to the liberal state?[20] On the one hand, calling for the removal of the cooperation requirement can sever protection from punishment and initially promises to construct a place for legal protection away from policing. A refusal pushes analysis out of the precompartmentalized limit the law sets in place where visa applicants are legal victims only when they are also racial figures of cooperative policing that anchors one's eligibility to even apply for visa status. But there still remains the need to find ways to work toward abolishing the racial and gendered figures tied to the victim subject in our analyses of law even while knowing that such categories will not fully leave the letter. Patricia Williams has written that the law might have a gender "and that gender might be a matter of words."[21] In some ways, I see the writing of experience as always reemerging in critical theory across a range of fields and conversations. We might consider critical race theory's argument for the relevance of race to the study of law as a set of questions about the role of experience and law. Here, some strands of critical race theory utilize lived experience to supplement the absence of racial representation in legal scholarship. While I depart slightly from this framework, I raise it here to demonstrate how theorizations of race and the power of law might always face difficulty tied to experience. Seeing, writing, or translating survivor experiences must be done carefully to guard against expectations of authenticity and the reproduction of harm, for example. Or to highlight critical theorizations of the subject against colonial knowledge production and neoliberal, pro-policing policy solutions.

Critical ethnic studies scholarship writes against the reliance on ethnic particularities that result in "food group" models of ethnic experience or racial identity that unwittingly result in appeals to universality.[22] For Asian American Studies and the study of law, the strength of this critique demonstrates how the supplemental use of racial particularity to stand in for knowledge about race results in empiricisms that can lend themselves to ways of knowing and writing that might reinforce the violence of law and assign value and worthiness to certain experiences. In other words, who has enough evidence to count as a proper victim under the law? As this book shows, legal protections produce a racial logic of value and worthiness that creates constraints and conditions of legal violence against survivors. Indeed, many liberal policy reforms mirror these knowledge formations by instilling institutional programs that change nothing of the core of the law while addressing race in an additive formulation. A critique against "food groups" while not distinctly theorizing violence is useful here in the sense that it assists in the pushback against the political reliance on bodies, voices, and experiences to provide the appropriate evidence for presumed ethnically relevant (culturally appropriate) political and scholarly questions. My aim is not to disregard lived experiences. Rather, I raise these questions about how experiences are referenced, conflated, or expected in order to put forward specific Asian American feminist theorizations developed through the ethnographic writing in this book.

Sora Han writes, "What makes critical race theory critical, in my mind, is its essentially theoretical orientation to law as a form and practice of writing."[23] Han's extension of critical race theory is an orientation toward law—in practice, institutions, and the letter—that pushes a poetic relation of histories, words, bodies, and ideas into the structure of law while law itself continually seeks to sever or to permanently bind.[24] I have tried to argue that in VAWA the bind is between protection and punishment through the use of policing to save women or the specific requirement to cooperate with police in order to receive temporary legal status. Thus, if we view "law as a form of writing and practice," as Han argues, we are able to see how VAWA is written to bind punishment to protection and give meaning to how legal practices are understood.[25] Further, political engagements of legal practice are ones that might "cast into poetic relation ideas, words, bodies, and histories that the structure of legal reason repeatedly severs . . . or obdurately binds."[26] What Han calls the "poetics of the plea" to the law is carried by those who have persisted into "law's language and its dreamwork" despite law's inherent limitations—and violence.[27]

In a reconsideration of the unrecognized empiricisms underlying formulations of race as a social construction, Denise Ferreira da Silva has argued that the racial is a modern category of being and that the primary effect is to produce universality itself. The racial is a strategy of power that we might consider to be at work already within law, particularly as an engulfment that can supplement (rather than defy) dominant narratives of modernity. As such, rather than render race to be outside the law, Ferreira da Silva argues instead that "*race difference* [is] resignified, introducing the idea that the *racial* only constitutes a strategy of power when *race difference* is invoked to justify exclusionary practices."[28] The consequence is that if one's racial difference is not visibly the cause of social exclusionary practices, then one's claim of harm has a far more difficult time being proven.[29] She further cautions against strands of both racial formation theory and critical race theory that may reduce the logic of race to be foreign to law or that are satisfied with defining the problem of law's power merely as dominance over the social. If race is viewed as a form of power only when it is excluded and thus only at the moment it is outside the law, this analysis not only misses the racial hierarchical categorizations produced by the category of the human as a strategy of power but also curtails and limits the political claims we imagine. Thus, this book argues that the legal subject of the crime victim produces a form of humanization through particular and uneven racial figures. The violence of law identified in this kind of critique is distinct from that which describes the dehumanization of law's effects. Without the critique of racial hierarchies that produce categories of the human through measurements of who is worthy or valued as the criminalized and the rescued, legal protection appears nonhierarchical, neutral, and seemingly nonviolent. When we are not only attuned to, but in tune with, feminist critiques of gender and sexual violence, whether in our political practice, collective relations, or engagements with law and policy, we come closer to understanding the limits of state power.

Legal Fiction and Ethnographic Impasse

All of the ethnographic stories and observations I present in this book are impasses, conversations along a path on which neither I nor the interlocutor came to an understanding but which nonetheless ended with our continued use of the same words. At first, these impasses were insignificant to my research. However, they eventually became central to my theorization because each impasse was a response to the relationship between the words advocates used as their own versus those of the law. Rather than assign an impasse to the shortcomings of ethnographic misrecognition, I seek to take up the spirit of this frustration through writing in hopes of building a relationship between the stakes of legal practice and the experience of writing about the law.[30] These difficulties that advocates had with depiction and interpretation were where I really saw the tensions and articulations between and within Asian American politics and feminist articulations emerge. While the ethnographic impasse is where most of my writing developed, I certainly did not start out with that. In fact, I simply began with questions about the logistical workings of law: How was a particular practice carried out in the day to day, who was involved, where did someone have to go, what paperwork was filed, what documents were procured, what phone calls did one make? In every conversation we all used the same words: *victim* or *survivor*, *coerced* and then *willing*, *culpable* but *cooperating*. I listened as advocates described in detail the process of law: conducting interviews and meetings with clients, preparing documentation, contacting state offices and partner organizations, and preparing an application.

It is almost impossible to write about antiviolence laws without referring to or writing with the word *victim*. My interest is not so much in reforming *victim* as a legal term or replacing it with a legal alternative but in theorizing the legal subject of the victim as exemplary of the racializing work of law. I listened as advocates would often pause to talk about the process of a law while attempting to avoid referencing their clients as victims, their clients' family members as perpetrators, or any activity marked as illegal or legal. At times, this was a political decision: "They are victims, but we don't think of them that way." But because most of our conversations were so focused on the step-by-step process, hesitancies, and outcomes of a client's application or case, all the attorneys I spoke with referred to their clients as victims when speaking about a legal process and then as persons when discussing a client's lived experiences regardless of law. Some viewed their advocacy work as permanently fixed—"we represent victims"—and articulated why they positioned their client services in this way in order to maintain relationships with law enforcement or because they believed the agendas of police served the needs of immigrant survivors. But in each of these conversations, attorneys also recognized and embraced that this placed their service work in tension with other Asian American or multiracial immigrant rights groups who actively campaigned for no cooperation with law enforcement or with Immigration and Customs Enforcement (ICE). While advocates I spoke with saw their nonprofit work as still separate from the state, some attorneys and case managers could not see any future where they did not have to position themselves as advocates of "victim's rights" agendas that remained neutral about policing, even if that meant distancing their work from that of other immigrant rights coalitions and prison abolition groups. For others, actively engaging antipolicing and antiprison analysis was fundamental to client services. These tensions are nothing new; I raise them here to underscore the ongoing stakes of what can and cannot pass through the word of law.

Robert Cover has argued that the power of law is not found in the behaviors of formal actors within institutions of law (i.e., judges and judicial interpretation) but rather in what he argues is the law's interpretative work in the word of law under which social agents operate.[31] Cover's emphasis on the *interpretative* as the structure and violence of law focuses on a legal phenomenon such as punishment—as that which cannot be understood simply as a metric of law (sentencing, for example). For Cover, law questions who may or may not be punished, and what force and application are legitimated, bringing together the social and the letter of law. However, Marianne Constable has argued that Cover, while focusing on the violence of the word in law, formulates violence as an occurrence only when law acts as the trigger point impressed onto the social, and thus the social as only reacting and responding to law. She further argues that Cover's analysis records the social only when voice or speech is actively making rights-based claims, only allowing for instances where social subjects have contact with law—speaking to the law, speech before the law—to then display evidence of law's "violence" or law's "justice." Constable argues instead that silence is not always an absence of voice but can be taken and used to construct consent or the legitimacy of power in the "temporality of claim and response that is the very condition, not only of voice, but also of law."[32] Thus, Constable argues that theorization must turn toward "law's silences," which can potentially reveal the relationship between law and language, and the limits of the social potential of what law is able to speak. If we examine language and how it matters to law, we can reveal "the pathologies and promises of modern law."[33]

Ethnographic impasses trace where the law has narrated itself to be nonviolent and humanitarian in order to remain silent on the racial violence of punishment toward the very subject it claims to both protect and expand. When I spoke with legal advocates, they interpreted their own practices, and these interpretations were produced both by the letter of law and through the site of the social, where immigrant presence and legally determined status were simultaneously rendered as "threats" to the state. To obtain protection for their clients, the articulations advocates provided demonstrate how survivors can only speak by matching their experiences to the racial figures the law demands, all the while having to strenuously distance themselves from the culpability of not having legal status and remaining within the nation-state. We might further consider an impasse to be a trace of what Angela Naimou calls the "debris" of legal personhood, an unstable translation of human beingness into the legal subject dependent on the law's "own object of recognition."[34] I locate the law's graphing of legal fictions (cooperation, mutual exchange, innocence) within the navigations that clients find themselves in, and the way this shapes what cannot be said and what must be said in order to be "successful" with law. They are impossible to understand in full without theorizing racializing figures. Colin Dayan has argued that the "improperly apprehended legal person" represents the subject of a legal right and duty that is stripped of such characteristics while remaining intact as a legal person. This kind of unpromising legal personhood shatters the stability of faith in the utility of the legal and political right and pushes us to contend with the "creation of a species of depersonalized persons."[35] Naimou's theorization in particular makes the case that legal personhood cannot be understood without contending with the legal fiction of personhood, or, namely, the legal slave as an unstable category that transforms itself into both self and property. As a figurative making that defined certain boundaries such as that between ghost and person, human and thing, legal personhood is unstable because of the *multiple* kinds of persons inscribed through legal code, rulemaking, and categories of law.[36]

My focus in this book is the site between the letter of law and legal practice where Asian undocumented and immigrant survivors in the US are configured into legal subjects of anti-Black racial figures coerced by the law's precursory requirements of eligibility. And so it is not the actual gift of citizenship but rather the potential precursor to legal personhood that I focus on, where the closest resemblance to a "right" or "rights-based claim" exists as a temporary form of protection more so than as a legal right. Rather than argue that legal ethnographies are able to unearth what is invisible or take up experience and storytelling as evidence of a particular legal discourse, I want to read ethnographic moments as themselves reflections both of and against law's letter and practice. Hershini Bhana Young has written, "Instead of the search for an object that leads to a subject, the scholar's search should be for a subject effect: a ghostly afterlife or a space of absence that is not empty but filled."[37]

Graphing Legal Fictions

JT: These are important issues. There was a Chinese girl, actually sisters, three of them . . . violence [occurred] in the same home from the same man. They were locked up, and he was the husband of all three sisters.

ME: What happened?

JT and I met in the Bay Area during my first year of ethnographic fieldwork. I saw her occasionally on days that I volunteered with her organization. During this particular month, I worked on a database categorizing service hours into funding streams, working on a fundraising project, and attending coalition meetings and network meetings with immigration and antiviolence organizations across the Bay Area. On this day, I was providing support for someone who managed the front desk and took calls in multiple languages, serving as a preintake first step for clients, family members, and anyone who might contact the organization. My conversation with JT came during a break in the day's work. I asked, How did she know the three sisters? JT responded that she did not know them and had instead generalized a story to me, one not unsimilar to something on television. Later, as I rode the Muni bus home, I retold this story to myself. But by the time I had traveled more than halfway across the Bay Bridge, I had completely lost my grasp of the situation. In her years with the organization, JT came across many stories of women both at the office and in spaces beyond it, many stories that she had already shared. Yet the one story she used as a follow-up to her statement "These are important issues" was not part of the organization's work. Was I less concerned now that the sisters were visible to me as fiction and, somehow, not legal victims; now that they were suddenly potential characters from a television show and not real women or real clients? And why did I feel so embarrassed? I was bothered and ashamed. I was perhaps even fearful that my facial expressions had given away the assumptions I held throughout this conversation, assumptions that I later came to realize were based on my desire to hear stories of a certain kind. I had expected for all my ethnographic exchanges to bring some story of truth, for my questions to enact and investigate, and for any answers or responses to be revealing. As I felt lost through the absence of some kind of evidence, I was also pushed to confront my own expectations and to think about the making of expectations through law's writing of women, the work of legal practice with women, and the truths that are expected.

Lila Abu-Lughod writes that stories do not "lift" or "get behind the veil" and do not merely reveal the unknown.[38] Rather, stories shift how we look at epistemological *objects* to begin with, be they unknown or familiar. Kirin Narayan argues that "finished texts," those polished and well-qualified ethnographies, are also, like novels, written through a narrative form.[39] To erase the borders that form between ethnography and fiction is to ignore the borders that exist within both genres and to abandon the potential theoretical richness that explorations into the making of such genres may provide. Narayan argues that the difference between ethnography and fiction emerges when researchers shift attention away from reading texts toward the practice of writing text. In many ways, feminist ethnographic writings have drawn our attention to this related difference between the blurred genres of ethnography and fiction, which I see reflected in legal ethnography as a methodology toward law and the grammar of the legal subject—legal fiction. For me, legal fiction is less about the notion that there might be a fictitious or false law, or a law that misrepresents or distorts the Real.[40] Rather, legal fictions are genres of the letter of the law itself; they are designed, and this design requires a legal subject that must constantly deny its bind to an object yet is already bound by the genre, by the writing and the material practice, of the law. Or more specifically in this book, the legal fictions of cooperation and mutual exchange in VAWA's immigration provisions establish a policing subject that must deny its bind to a policed object. Legal fiction is a genre of law itself; it materializes in the letter of the law and in practice through the constant writing of legal subjects and the racial figures they produce. Legal fictions might matter because they present us with violences that do not initially appear, they might identify the grammar of the legal subject that requires our critique, and they may provide ways to write and think through the relationship between laws and our lives. To begin here, rather than with an effort to reform or refine evidentiary violence, is to practice a refusal.

Kamala Visweswaran has further argued that acts of feminist ethnography might involve silence, that the speaker is already representing conflicting and multiple positions and may refuse to speak, or choose to speak temporally.[41] These insights push us to consider legal ethnography as a feminist ethnography. Ethnographic writing might know about the everyday workings of the legal system, about how legal institutions shape people's lives; we learn about the ways in which law is understood and interpreted by those who seek it. But rarely are we ever prepared *to unlearn* the ethnographic moments we have just participated in. That is, if we are jolted into moments in which the stories we hear reveal themselves to be without the evidence we expected, what does this mean for the study of law and ethnographic research? Feminist of color approaches to experience in ethnographic writing might take up experience as a form of racial critique rather than evidence of the omniscience of law. If instead of evidence as the singular truth-telling source that unveils law through the suffering of women, or the reverse as the universal liberation from pain, we might consider feminist ethnographic approaches to be ones that do not seek the damaged victim's voice but instead listen to the already sexualized and racialized logics within law's own writing. The problem with victimhood is not merely that it is dominated by white women's narratives or white domestic spaces but that white supremacy disregards gender and sexual violence as symptomatic of state violence, structures or racial capitalism, war, imperialism, and colonialism.

2

Making the Undocumented Crime Victim

COOPERATION, MODEL MINORITY, AND POLICING
AS MUTUAL EXCHANGE

"The abuse is not enough." DJ repeated these words over and over as she described the process of helping her client Kay apply for U nonimmigrant status, a temporary form of legal status commonly referred to as the U visa.[1] Legislated through the 2000 Victims of Trafficking and Violence Protection Act (VTVPA) and reauthorization of (VAWA), U status was promising because it offered relief to survivors who did not have authorized immigration status or were at risk of falling out of status, whereas prior forms of legal relief were available only to those who were married to citizens or legal permanent residents or who had been sponsored by citizens or legal permanent residents.[2] The U was a temporary legal status available to qualifying applicants if they became certified as "willing" and able to assist with law enforcement. This requirement for *cooperation* is central and produces a specific bind between punishment and protection that hinges on particular racial figures and legal subject positions. DJ had just begun working with potential applicants for the U visa in the San

Francisco Bay Area. I continued to ask, What wasn't enough? Was it the evidence or something else about Kay or the person who had caused her harm? The violence Kay had already experienced would never be enough if she could not also demonstrate a will to cooperate with policing and obtain a signed certification form of that willingness from a qualifying agency—often a policing or law enforcement agency. Kay was a Chinese undocumented survivor from Vietnam; she was staying at a women's shelter in the Bay Area and had gone back to the shelter several times in the past year. Advocates at the shelter knew that Kay was a survivor of both gender-based violence and the violence of the immigration system itself, which left little room for undocumented people to leave violent conditions if they were dependent on a person or a workplace for their legal status. To help Kay with all of these elements of survival, shelter advocates contacted DJ, and U status seemed like a potential solution. But despite all the paperwork Kay had from emergency rooms, the shelter, and law enforcement documenting violence over several years, DJ was unsure if she should lead Kay down the path of hoping for this form of legal relief.

In this legal scheme, a certain kind of violence occurs when survivors become legible only if they are a particular kind of victim of a crime and, even further, must make their experiences match up to an interiority that is measured by the law. At the time of my interview with DJ, it had been close to a decade since U status had first been introduced in 2000, but the rules and regulations for the application process were still widely unknown by many advocates I spoke with. To help clients apply for U status, advocates had to prepare a packet of required immigration forms, certifications, and supporting evidence and then submitted those by mail to service centers administered by the Office on Violence Against Women and the United States Citizenship and Immigration Service. In the early 2000s, DJ shared that it was not clear which forms should be submitted, what additional documentation was required, and the certification forms that needed to be signed by law enforcement agencies were not readily available. Some advocates created their own certification forms in hopes that law enforcement would sign them. Even later once these forms were available, it was still particularly challenging to obtain signed certifications from police agencies who were hesitant to assist victim-related concerns that involved undocumented and immigrant survivors. In addition, DJ encountered many law enforcement agencies who sidestepped or delayed certification because they were hesitant or refused to sign certification forms. DJ learned that another attorney had contacted the Office on Violence Against Women and the US Citizenship and Immigration Services (USCIS) office to obtain the actual document for certification. I interviewed DJ one other time; although she was unable to share the specifics of Kay's application process, I was informed that a year had passed, and Kay was still waiting.

U status is commonly referred as a "U visa" in both state documents, interviews I conducted with advocates, and in political debates. I will continue to refer to the "U visa" or "U status" interchangeably. The U visa is unlike a typical visa that allows someone outside the nation-state to temporarily enter. Rather, the U is a form of temporary legal status designed for those already within the nation-state. The U visa is narrated as a solution designed to rescue and save vulnerable communities, and this narration largely relies on the sign of woman as the figure of feminized victimhood. Because of this, the U visa can fall under the radar of political criticism of the violence of the American immigration system. Whereas deportation and detention constitute particular legible forms of racial violence, protections such as the U visa are easily seen as exceptions to the broader violence of our current immigration system because they function as inclusions rather than exclusions. This chapter demonstrates otherwise: Legal protections such as U status place gender at the center of broader relationships of violence against migrant communities that occur between immigration enforcement and policing because of the required certification of cooperation with mechanisms of punishment that applicants must successfully obtain in order to be eligible to apply for protection. If the problem of the U visa is understood only as an administrative failure, then its function as a policing solution is left untouched, and the conditions migrant survivors face are easily ignored when they successfully become the recipients of solutions, receiving protection. Overseen by the political work of liberalism underlying the modern state formation, this formulation produces a social condition shaped by the legal apparatuses at play whereby the legal subject of the U visa's "undocumented crime victim" is simultaneously the object of projection and the subject that unfurls punishment. That is, while the terminology of victim is often used interchangeably with woman or person, I argue instead that the *undocumented crime victim* is not a person but rather a legal subject position. Here, the legal subject relies on racial and gendered figures to provide meaning making, and survivors must match their experiences to these figures in order to be eligible to apply for U status. This chapter argues that the U visa's legal scheme is a racial assemblage of the human cooperator intended to improve policing, and if that expectation is met, protection is then made available to survivors—a *temporary* protection.

In this chapter I discuss the legal fiction of mutual exchange and the U visa as exemplary of the good/bad immigrant paradigm, a collapse of that paradigm, and an example of assimilationist model minority myth discourse as a criminalizing framework. Further, I discuss how the figure of the cooperator as a category of the human establishes hierarchies between those who are willing, credible, and able to serve the betterment of policing and those who are not. If undocumented survivors are already held culpable because their presence is punished by immigration law, then cooperation emerges under conditions more similar to coercion than to an active exchange. Because applicants for U visas are simultaneously the objects of protection and the subjects used by law to unfurl punishment, their constant shuttling between innocence and culpability makes possible their very eligibility for protection while simultaneously foreclosing any legality outside the narrative device of mutual exchange. Not only should this exchange be viewed as coerced, but its expectations also demand a permanent resolution to improve policing yet provide only a temporary protection to survivors. I present ethnographic impasses drawn from stories shared by advocates working with Asian American survivors attempting to apply for U visas. Their stories and interpretations reflected both alignments and impasses between the letter of the law and the practice of advocacy, or what was expected of survivors and advocates. How did U visa rules narrate who an applicant was or ought to be, and what terms did advocates use to explain the legal subjects their clients were expected to position themselves within? Often, advocates would pause or correct themselves as they talked about cooperation between survivors and police, or the political tensions law unfurled between immigrant rights advocates who critiqued cooperation and antiviolence advocates assisting survivors with cooperation requirements.

This book contributes an analysis of immigration to the existing literature on VAWA's pro-policing agenda.[3] During the era of 1990s neoliberal policy reform, the politics of the mainstream antiviolence movement aligned with policies and laws expanding policing, prisons, immigration enforcement and rolling back welfare along racial and gendered lines. As a result of new federal legislation and funding, the politics of *safety for survivors* became one of many litmus tests to establish the legitimacy of law enforcement *public safety* agendas that criminalized poor communities of color by increasing the policing of race, gender, and sexuality. There is a historical tension between "public safety" and survivor safety—the safety and needs of communities who are most vulnerable and with the least resources. For survivors who are spectacularized by public safety agendas, yet who belong to communities that are policed, surveilled, and targeted, their needs and their communities' futures can never fully be a part of public safety political agendas. Mimi Kim has shown that the expansion of law enforcement resulted in the slow "carceral creep" of punishment ideologies within antiviolence advocacy programs that found themselves grappling with entangled relationships with law enforcement even as many of them also worked with communities often targeted by law enforcement.[4] Writing against public safety agendas as well, Christina Hanhardt argues that queer political movements that call for safe spaces in cities and neighborhoods have also had to contend with the violence of policing as well as the normative politics of safety that emerge in response to such policing.[5] Further, Jane Stoever argues that an ongoing and specific agenda of *politicized safety* submerges other policy efforts to address broader economic, housing, and related needs beyond overly funded law enforcement responses to violence.[6]

Beth Richie has argued that the building of prisons and policing under the guise of rescuing women renders Black gender and sexuality as raw material for criminalization. In this formulation, Black women are never able to emerge as legal subjects of proper victimhood.[7] If laws, policies, and institutions of punishment have already targeted Black communities, migrants of color, Indigenous peoples and places, and queer and gender-nonconforming people and relations, then no legal protection can ever be extended to survivors of gender and sexual violence who are part of these communities.[8] How do we understand the U visa within this larger context of racial criminalization? Rather than isolate or exceptionalize this form of protection, this chapter identifies what makes possible the racial and gendered logic of U status whereby only undocumented survivors are required to obtain a certification of cooperation with law enforcement. What are the expectations put in place for survivors, and how does the requirement to assist with policing shape the terms of advocacy and political discourses that relate to criminalization? Abolition feminist and queer of color community organizers, artists, scholars, and writers have continued to argue that the presence of police materializes in multiple forms that must all be accounted for; whether some experience harm because of police or some do not, these all exemplify how legal protections are tied to legal punishment in uneven and competing ways that must be abolished.[9] The making of noncitizen survivors into "cooperators" with logics of policing is one of these uneven and competing sites that must be interrogated.

Cooperator

I first learned about the U visa while conducting research in the San Francisco Bay Area with an Asian American domestic violence organization focused on policy and outreach. As part of my work, I attended meetings with the organization's coalition members, who were mostly eager for the rollout of the U visa as a possible new tool for clients. The coalition itself was a group that gathered to collaborate on projects initiated through federal and state grants focused on technical assistance trainings among attorneys, case managers, social workers, and administrators from county and state agencies. The U visa had promise. But it is important to note that this feeling of promise was in part a response to the growing deportation infrastructure of this moment. Early in my fieldwork, I met KS, who worked at multiple locations across the Bay Area as part of her legal advocacy. When we first spoke, I was most struck by how frequently law enforcement agencies appeared in her stories. Without hiding my shock, I asked KS about her thoughts, and she shared, "What else can I do? What do you expect me to do?" and went on to articulate a series of frustrations based in her own experiences with the criminal legal system, her clients' frustrations, and frustration with my actual question. This was the kind of moment ethnography tends to ignore, dreads, and would rather avoid, for it appears as an impasse devoid of dialogue and understanding. But such moments present a theoretical reopening between political reimagining and legal practice, the way we write about the law, and the law's own telling of who immigrant women and their advocates ought to be.

Throughout the year I thought often about KS's question. What begins to unfurl when the few legal options available are bound within institutions of punishment and agencies of enforcement? What modes of participation does the law expect of those who engage in this relationship? This identifiable limit and its almost defeating frustration make this moment paramount to critical thought. We might take up this frustration—namely, the frustration with laws that promise to protect immigrant women only when they and their legal advocates participate in institutions of criminalization—as a call that ethnographic writing can respond to. Can we configure an analysis specifically around the formation of legal protection—who is protected, what damage they must undergo to be worthy of protection, who even qualifies as properly damaged, and then, further, what must be exchanged to receive that protection? Such questions have long been addressed by feminist and queer of color organizers and advocates, whose analyses have made possible a host of questions now referenced and used in critical theory. In particular, writers, thinkers, and organizers centering gender-based violence in their work have argued that interpersonal violence within communities cannot be understood outside forms of state violence and that state violence is not abstracted but rather centered and maintained through gender and sexual violence.[10] Further, laws that promise safety and reduce violence by instilling legal punishment and increased policing do more to establish what Chinyere Oparah has called the state as protector than to reduce or end gender-based violence.[11] It is this categorical assignment of protection to law that I wish to pause and engage with as part of the larger path toward abolishing the presence of punishment.

I later met ML, a family law and immigration law attorney from the Bay Area. ML explained the mechanics of the U visa to me and then began discussing cooperation in ways that I had not heard before. ML articulated a struggling relationship that formed among her, her clients, and local law enforcement:

> Can you imagine having to work under that kind of rubric that gives them so much power over your client? If your client said no to cooperation one day because they were feeling bad, or they were scared, is it fair for them to get denied a visa just because of that? Law enforcement will say, Well, she did not cooperate. When I first started working... I couldn't get a certification for my client [or even] a letter stating that they had no [criminal] record.... It's a problem.... A lot of police departments do not want to help us with immigration cases; they simply do not want to help us....

"Can you imagine?" she asked, describing the pressures and constraints she faced from law enforcement. As part of each U visa application, ML is required to submit a certification form that her client must obtain from a qualifying agency to guarantee that cooperation is part of the deal. She asked, What if a client says no to cooperating one day? After asking, "Can you imagine?" she began to concretely map out how the visa would shape the future of her clients and her work in ways that were not present before. ML argued that the rubric had so much power over her clients that it pushed them to cooperate in order to be eligible to apply for the visa—not to receive, but just to apply. While a client perhaps could say no, ML's story also reveals how impossible it is for an immigrant woman without legal status to say no to cooperation. This also reflects ML's understanding of her own role. While she asked me to imagine what would happen to her client, her reflections also included an interpretation of her own advocacy work if she were to question cooperation one day as well.

Undocumented immigrant women who seek to leave conditions of violence face many concerns: fears for their own safety and the safety of their children and other family members; difficult economic conditions, potential deportation, lack of shelter, and trauma; language accessibility; and fear of law enforcement or state agencies. The U visa is not primarily designed to address any of these concerns. Instead, it temporarily removes the burden of legal status but only for the duration of the visa. It also puts in place other demands—such as the new requirement of cooperation with law enforcement—that inspire their own forms of apprehension. As ML shared, "It's a problem.... A lot of police departments do not want to help us with immigration cases"; the police are not invested in the U visa for its role in immigrants' lives but for its purpose of assisting law enforcement in the successful prosecution of criminal activity—a project that expands much further into policing and surveillance. ML continued, "The state wants law enforcement to have a hand in determining whether a case is *real* ... and they want to deter thousands of [people] from asking for U visas." But what does the law possibly allow to be "real" in the U visa scheme? Not only does the law expect undocumented survivors to play a role in keeping the larger public safe (while struggling to find safety for themselves), but they must serve as human deterrents as well.

The *FBI Law Enforcement Bulletin* has described the goal of the U visa in this way: "Law enforcement personnel strive for strong connections with all citizens. In pursuit of this goal, striking an appropriate balance—one that punishes wrongdoers while protecting victims—can present a challenge. One way that officers not only can foster better relationships with immigrant communities but also increase offender accountability, promote public safety, and help ensure that crimes translate into convictions is to promote awareness of the U visa, which provides important immigration benefits to cooperating crime victims."[12]

The *FBI Law Enforcement Bulletin* is a regular trade magazine for employees and agencies.[13] In the 2009 article, the *Bulletin* suggests that immigrants' cooperation will allow the law to do its part by addressing a specific challenge—that immigrant women are afraid to call the police. In response, the law seeks to strike "an appropriate balance—one that punishes wrongdoers while protecting victims"—and to strengthen "the ability of law enforcement agencies to investigate and prosecute." The challenge described here is not defined by the historical conditions of state violence against immigrants that have led, and continue to lead, to fear of police. Instead, the report suggests that because immigrants may hesitate to cooperate, law enforcement agents are unable to do their job of punishing "wrongdoers" and protecting "victims." The *Bulletin* argues that by fostering trust and active cooperation between immigrant women and law enforcement, the U visa will help tease out the good from the bad, the victims from the wrongdoers. In effect, it suggests that providing legal status to undocumented women is unconditionally temporary and that this temporality is tied not to the shifting conditions of women's lives but rather to the time needed to strengthen the police state.

Further, the visa was described in this way: "The fear of deportation can cause immigrant communities to cut themselves off from police and not offer information about criminal activity, even when victimized. Consequently, predators remain on the street, emboldened because they know they can strike with a degree of impunity. As a result, societies face increased crime, including serious offenses, and the perpetrators victimize and endanger everyone, not just illegal immigrants."[14] The narrative explicitly writes out other experiences of fear, for example, if a client feared what would happen if they *could not* cooperate one day, if they held an awareness that they were both innocent and culpable clients whose relationship to the state did not automatically result in a steadfast desire to prosecute members of their own communities. In the *Bulletin*, however, immigrant women's fear of deportation is marked as irrational (they "cut themselves off... even when victimized") and also misplaced (the police are not to be feared). The supposed consequence that the *Bulletin* describes is a state of fear the entire public experiences, not just noncitizens, furthering the narrative that immigrant women's lives are of value only when tied to the betterment of public safety overall.

What, then, of undocumented immigrant survivors who hesitate to cooperate? Of those who refuse? Are their fears and struggles irrational and misplaced because they hesitate to cooperate with the police? Indeed, the U visa does nothing to change laws that make immigrants vulnerable in the first place and leaves the material conditions of culpability still very much embodied by undocumented immigrant women, even as they apply for a visa they are not sure they will receive. In contrast to the *Bulletin*'s definition of a one-dimensional fear, undocumented and immigrant survivors will also fear being forced or required to provide help *to* law enforcement, being made into enforcers of the law, having no room to say no to cooperation, and becoming defined by this particular relationship with the law. Incorporating victimhood is a central component of community policing, framed as the opportunity for victims to be partners, develop community problem-solving, and collapse barriers between enforcement and the enforced.[15]

As I argue, the U visa renders immigrant survivors as both objects of targeted protection and subjects whom the law enlists to cooperate in the unleashing of criminal enforcement. This makes evident the purpose of the U visa: not protecting undocumented women from violence but improving and strengthening law enforcement. At the same time, the schema of cooperation frames this relationship as based on the agreement of a "willing" crime victim, rather than the coercive condition of undocumented immigrant women. Thus, the law's investment in innocence is almost superfluous to the mechanism of the U visa. But what the U visa does accomplish is to swallow immigrant women's lives with the legal fiction of a *mutual exchange* where, in the absence of a shared goal between law enforcement and immigrant women, a narrative logic of "better relationships" is still somehow produced.

In 1994 VAWA's first set of immigration provisions focused on survivors whose legal status was dependent on their relationship with a US citizen or legal permanent resident (LPR). The act allowed survivors to apply for a waiver of inadmissibility which would allow them to adjust their legal status on their own and potentially remove any legal dependency on a person causing them harm. Undocumented survivors were not eligible for any of these initial immigration provisions. Without a legal relationship to a citizen or LPR, such as marriage, for example, survivors could not be legible as victims and thus not eligible for VAWA immigration–related protections. When VAWA was reauthorized in 2000, policy advocates and service providers working with mainstream antiviolence movements pushed for the inclusion of new provisions designed specifically for undocumented communities. Ultimately, legislation created a new type of nonimmigrant legal status, or a category of legal status that is intended to be only temporary without any pathway to permanency—the U visa.[16] The U visa does not function as a typical visa for crossing nation-state borders but rather adjusts the legal status of someone who already resides within. This legal protection addressed the problem of legal status only for those who could qualify as victims of a specific list of qualifying crimes. Indeed, when it comes to the U visa, the presence of a qualifying crime must precede the existence of harm in a potential applicant's life. Thus, the making and unmaking of legal status unfolds within the apparatus of racial meaning making in not only protection but also punishment. In such relations, the withholding of legal status as well as the promise of delivering legal status demands a particular victim figure; that figure must succeed in navigating and fulfilling the expectations of law.

Most notably, the U visa included a very distinct requirement for certification of cooperation with policing. No other provision within VAWA required survivors to cooperate with law enforcement in this way. And this requirement is the site through which protection and punishment require analyses of race and the liberal subject of law. If critiques of VAWA's policing history place less emphasis on immigration provisions, this renders such provisions as purely beneficial and necessary in order to obtain something for categories that would otherwise have nothing. What follows is an analytical line of exceptionalism whereby mutual exchange and cooperation become acceptable. As I have argued, mutual exchange is a legal fiction when someone has little choice when trying to avoid the state violence of deportation while also surviving gender-based violence in their lives—and to appear as a credible cooperator at the same time. Here, legal protection does begin with the need for health, housing, mental health, financial support, childcare, transportation, food, clothing, or family support. Legal protection for noncitizen survivors would look very different if it began with the actual things survivors needed to be safe and to thrive. Instead, the protection begins first and foremost as a key tool designed to improve law enforcement "detection, investigation, or prosecution."[17]

Currently, a maximum of ten thousand U visas can be granted per year for principal applicants; there is no cap for those with derivative status or family members who may qualify.[18] A successful application grants temporary legal status for a possible four-year period, potential work eligibility, and potential nonimmigrant status for family members, and if those who receive U status can prove that cooperation with law enforcement has not been "unreasonably refused," then they may be eligible for green card status at a later date.[19] Additionally, applicants are eligible only if they agree to cooperate with law enforcement in criminal prosecutions and prove that their willingness to cooperate is in "good faith." They must also approach a qualifying agency (in most cases law enforcement) and obtain a certification (form I-918B) from a certified official, confirming their willingness to be helpful in the detection, investigation, or prosecution of a qualifying criminal activity.[20] We should read the U visa as a protection that is prefigured by VAWA's earlier legacy and formulation of legal punishment as a necessary means to ending gender-based violence, which places high stakes on the requirement for cooperation as a prerequisite for temporary legal status.[21]

Most applicants do not come to know about the U visa on their own. The attorneys and social workers I spoke with often encountered potential applicants through referrals and would not have worked on U visa applications otherwise. Some were part of federally funded networks among nonprofit organizations, hospitals, law enforcement agencies, and social services agencies. Through these networks, certain survivors who could qualify to apply for U status were referred to attorneys. In every interview I conducted, I always asked what cooperation looked like, and attorneys would generally describe the different possible outcomes of an application process, or what documentation the law would expect. Every interview provided abstracted details from the (then) vague set of U visa administrative regulations. But one morning I showed up for a small volunteer event at the Asian American legal center where I had volunteered and interviewed several advocates. That morning, as we moved boxes and furniture and painted walls, I stood next to CP, an attorney I had interviewed several months prior. As we painted, I turned to her and asked how she thought the interview went, and she immediately said, "I have a different answer for your question about cooperation. Cooperation—it's nothing." We continued painting, and she shared that most applicants were already in some kind of situation where they had come into contact with law enforcement; they were already cooperating in some way, or had been made to. And she then described the certification requirement as a redundancy. For CP, this conversation provided an opportunity for her to deemphasize the certification requirement because she felt this requirement was administratively insignificant and reflected little legal change. For me, this moment brought forward an ethnographic impasse that heightened and overemphasized the significance of the law's making of survivors into human cooperators if the actual material conditions or relations of cooperation were "nothing." This was the stuff, so to speak, that constituted what cooperation was—nothing.

Survivors who apply for U status and any individuals who can qualify as family members and receive derivative status from a U petitioner must first demonstrate victimhood resulting from one or more forms of criminal activity. Currently, there are thirty-one forms of designated criminal activity that qualify. Some may have experienced prior deportation, removal, past criminalization, or may have crossed a nation-state border without authorization, acts that would legally render them inadmissible. A waiver of inadmissibility would allow survivors to receive advance permission to potentially remain in the United States. An application must also include material demonstrating suffering in the form of substantive physical or mental abuse directly caused by one of the thirty-one forms of qualifying criminal activity. Most of the attorneys and social workers I interviewed assisted their clients with the written personal statement to demonstrate harm, submission of any additional supporting documentation, and procurement of documentation certifying information about a qualifying criminal activity and having cooperated in assisting or being willing to assist in the prosecution of that activity with either law enforcement or prosecutors of a case. These materials are mailed to one of (currently) two processing centers and reviewed by USCIS.

From 2012 to 2018, 68 percent of petitioners identified Mexico as their place of birth, 31 percent of petitioners were identified as men, and a decreasing number of petitioners were identified as women (dropping from 69 percent in 2012 to 58 percent in 2018).[22] The demographic profile of U visa petitioners, of applicants who are then either accepted or denied, will always shift, but I raise these demographics to highlight that even though women are decreasingly able to actually petition—to apply—for U nonimmigrant status, the spectacle of rescuing the feminine continues to shape the discourse around this legal protection and drives the racializing logics of its tie to punishment via policing. The majority of those who petitioned for a visa (79 percent) did not have lawful legal status, nor did derivatives (65 percent), and an estimated 13 percent of principal petitioners and 8 percent of family members were already in removal proceedings when the application was filed. As reported by USCIS, 20 percent of approved

U visa petitions were from individuals who required a waiver of inadmissibility because they lacked identification documents or were undocumented. From USCIS's perspective, this 20 percent demonstrates that the law is "working" because it has resulted in encouraging this percentage of inadmissible people to cooperate with law enforcement.[23] We might view this percentage differently, as a group of survivors who had already endured immigration enforcements that render them unauthorized or inadmissible because they migrated for life-changing conditions or because laws changed and made them suddenly vulnerable due to their immigration status.

The Legal Fiction of Mutual Exchange

In 2010 I met SP, an attorney in the East Bay Area with a legal center serving women from both Latinx and Asian immigrant communities. SP helped clients seek asylum, worked with refugees, and provided assistance to a number of women who sought help from the law as survivors of domestic violence. She spoke at length about shifting relationships with law enforcement—more than she ever would have imagined when she first started serving clients. SP was clear that the only strategy in place for legal relief was a victim-based one and that she did what was best for her clients. While she worked within this strategy, she also wrestled with its implications. When I asked her about the U visa's complexities, SP shared this interpretation: "We have clients who feel, 'I was a crime victim, and I have no status. If there was amnesty, I would go for amnesty, but being a crime victim is the only way available to me, and so I have to do it.' [I think] it's absurd that people have to use this strange thing. Because the U visa is a bizarre way of relating to the community by saying, 'You can't get status until you say that somebody did something to you,' and that's a weird way to conceive of oneself."

In her interpretation of the U visa, SP began with an articulation of coercion—"being a crime victim is the only way ... so I have to do it." She continued to discuss "this strange thing" wherein immigrant women have to say that someone did something to them in order to obtain temporary legal status, not freedom or liberation or a sense of self. This is deeply profound, and it pushes us to think about how the visa shifts understandings of the self as reflected in the relationships between advocates and clients. Under the U visa, women live within a narrative logic that allows them to be innocent if they are victims of crime enacted by a person but disallows their recognition as communities experiencing harm from the state and its violences. This is the "absurd" thing that SP described her clients as feeling when they must enforce the law against their own community.

As SP explains, this is "a weird way to conceive of oneself." But if someone needs a U visa, it is the only way to conceive of one's self. The conception is in many ways a strategy of survival for someone who has to become innocent (but only as a victim) at the very same moment the law denies that they were ever anything but innocent to begin with (because of their immigration status). Fictionalized, then, as willing and empowered to cooperate and serve the purposes of police, immigrant women's interior experiences are never realized outside of this constant need to demonstrate how undamaged they are in order to be credible as willing human cooperators amid interagency shifts in law enforcement. In the U visa scheme, there is no future for survivors of violence outside of the racial violence of policing and punishment against their own communities and others.

Rather, the racial figure of the cooperator is a category of the human that creates hierarchies of value and worth. While providing a pathway for inclusion in the nation-state, the U visa does nothing to actually change the terms by which immigrant women are controlled by US immigration law and fear punishment because of legal status. This is troubling. We are pushed to look more deeply at the racial logics of inclusion that drive the U visa's promise to protect undocumented women. While inclusion in the nation-state is rarely the site where the violence of law is theorized (in comparison to legal exclusions), we cannot afford to continue rendering legal inclusion as a nonviolent, gender- and race-neutral path, particularly as the convergence of immigration law and criminal enforcement is made evident by legal innovations like the U visa.[24] For example, Jin Haritaworn, Adi Kuntsman, and Silvia Posocco have argued that the modern liberal state will constantly attempt to fold homonormative injured white subjects and only improperly include queer of color bodies through *murderous inclusions*.[25] Eric Stanley, writing on trans/queer ungovernability under contemporary conditions of "atmospheric violence," argues that one element of state violence is the constant reforming of inclusions.[26]

The U visa makes evident a particular strategy of state violence in which immigrant women's lives are used for state survival, even as women themselves seek legal assistance for their own survival. In no way does the visa work to amend the laws that actually construct the violence of immigration enforcement; rather, it seeks to provide an opening for immigrant women through a shaky expectation that they will be both innocent objects of the law and subjects who must disavow punishment the law has already placed on them. In other words, immigrant women appear as ostensibly willing subjects who cooperate because of their status as victims *innocent* of crime. However, immigrant women come before the law to remedy their immigration legal status, for which they have already been held as culpable, not innocent. Without this legal move to sidestep already existing violence that survivors undergo because of the state's own enforcement and borders, the visa's fiction of mutual exchange is undercut when the coercive conditions that undocumented immigrant women undergo reveal they have no choice but to apply for a visa because of their culpability for remaining within the nation-state without legal status. They are made into consenting mutual co-operators purportedly willing to advance punishment in exchange for protection when they themselves already face forms of punishment by the law of the state and not only at the hands of an abuser. In other words, the anxiety within the law emerges as the U visa scheme aims to erase tensions between the protection of innocence and the punishment that the subject of innocence already faces because of larger structures of state violence. The disavowal of state violence enacted through the enforcement of legal status must continually distance itself from the innocence established by the legal figure of the undocumented crime victim as a cooperator. This figure plays a role in unfurling other forms of policing, punishment, and criminalization racially assembled through protection as a liberal genre of the human. As such, the figure of the cooperator does not work to dehumanize those who are not protected but rather to enact the violence of protection *by* humanizing those who successfully fold into the position of innocent credibility for policing. And all the while, they are living under the terror of vulnerability already imposed on them by law's restrictions and expulsions of those without legal status or in vulnerable positions as noncitizens. In the U visa scheme, legal violence is enacted not when migrant survivors are denied a visa but when they are shuttled back and forth between conditions of innocence and culpability for cooperation with policing.

The violence of this legal scheme is entirely a racial condition—it is produced, enforced, and maintained by the political inclusion of innocence. Innocence as the not deviant, the not culpable, the not criminal, is underwritten by the permanence of what is to (always) be criminalized through racial difference. Further, *legal* protection is an outgrowth of the liberal rights-bearing state and not organic to collective movements and community organizing. When understood this way, the scale of political violence in law is not that communities are never properly protected but rather that they face the violence of law's desire to selectively match them to proper victim figures used to unfurl punishment. Further, the universalism of only the most extreme and exceptional forms of violence is enough to be properly injured, but never for those already marked through criminalization, deviance, or the violence of the law itself. Thus, rather than view innocence to be simply mistaken or racially misrepresented for some and not others, we might view political identities and political discourses tied to frameworks of innocence as sites from which violences unfold by seemingly neutral institutions like "community policing," militarized humanitarianisms—and mutual exchange. Ruth Wilson Gilmore has argued that the "sentimental political assertion" of innocence achieves significance as an exception to carcerality and the false reassurance that the criminals are criminals and the rest are not.[27] Gilmore writes that this "sentimental political assertion ... depends on the figuring of a laboring victim."[28] The persistent revival that promises to negate the form of carcerality in this emerging exceptionalism is not merely appealing because it is possible but, Gilmore writes, because it is *abundantly* possible by always negating itself, in new forms and with no fixed end. We might consider the legal subject of the undocumented crime victim to be one kind of laboring victim. The display of gender and sexual violence as a social problem is no stranger to the abundance of victimhood that colors policing as rescue.

In the original congressional debate over proposed provisions like the U visa, the Subcommittee on Immigration and Claims within the Committee of the Judiciary held several hearings on the Battered Immigrant Women Protection Act, the subsection of VAWA's reauthorization in 2000 introducing the U visa. Representative Lamar Smith argued that the U visa had to include a component requiring cooperation and described this cooperation requirement as an official marker that would assuredly end violence in women's lives. Leslye Orloff with Legal Momentum, an organization that pushed numerous pieces of legislation on violence against women, testified at this hearing. Orloff responded to Smith with a critique of cooperation: "Lots of times you have women who may want to cooperate but are legitimately terrified that if in fact they cooperate with law enforcement they will get killed. And so, I don't think it would be wise to have any piece of legislation that requires such cooperation, and, in fact, original VAWA did not for that reason."[29] Countering Senator Smith's argument that without cooperation the cycle would never end, Orloff presented the alternative—death.

Good/Bad Immigrant as Criminalization and the Model Minority Myth

In February 2013, Senator Diane Black of Tennessee, a proponent of militarized policing and harsher penalties for migration, introduced the U Visa Reform Act of 2013. Rather than eliminate the visa, Black proposed, "While a criminal act against any individual in this country is inexcusable and reprehensible regardless of immigration status, it is not good immigration policy to staple green cards to police reports for those in the country illegally."[30] The bill aimed to make the U visa truly temporary by eliminating the opportunity for visa holders to apply for green cards, removing eligibility for family members, reducing the categories of criminality that qualify for eligibility, and reducing the duration of the visa. "We are a nation of immigrants," Black argued, but also a "nation built upon the respect for the rule of law" that should grant only those who "follow the law" and "want to contribute to the betterment of our nation" the opportunity to do so. Black's deployment of national unification serves as the mechanism of legibility for racialized and sexualized legal subjects through what Chandan Reddy has argued is the state's success in establishing itself as a secured and safe distributor of legal entitlements, recognized as the ongoing neoliberal narratives of the welfare state's framing of the deserving and the worthy along racial and gendered lines.[31] It is important to note that Black does not reject the U visa. She is in fact invested in maintaining the visa as a form of temporary inclusion, insofar as it allows her to set forth a narrative reinscribing the law's avowal of its ability to clearly distinguish the "bad" immigrants from the "good." In this way, Black envisions a cooperative future that rationalizes the nation-state's purported need to use immigrant women as enforcers in the nation's defense of itself. Even when the fairness of this cooperation has been questioned in public discourse, it has been suggested that immigrant women may be getting too much out of the deal.

The U visa is a form of legal violence not because its terms are insufficient, unfair, or unequal, but because this law continues to push women into the purest form of innocence, because of the law's demand for innocence untethered to culpability as the basis for legitimizing their worthiness of legal status. This mobilizes a story that only innocent immigrants are worthy of protection and granted the gift of legal status—the ideal exchange. To be innocent here is to be an undocumented crime victim defined through a willingness to cooperate that is abstracted into the purportedly nonviolent effect of immigration law. The law removes itself from any responsibility for the broader conditions that survivors undergo as they are coerced to move between two legal figures—from the culpable stance (at risk due to lack of legal status) to the enforcer who must cooperate with the law in order to grapple with the pressures of maintaining this position of pure innocence that masks the legal fiction of mutual exchange. While this potentially results in the delivery of U legal status, it does not address the conditions women undergo. Further, discourses such as Black's are afforded opportunities to restage the legal fiction of a fairer exchange between the state and immigrant women where only "those who want to contribute to the betterment of our nation" are offered visas—a scenario in which immigrant women can never win because their culpability always conditions the terms by which they are rendered willing enough as cooperators. Black produces a future where if survivors accept the visa, they can only become legal subjects who enforce prosecution. This is a condition that we cannot afford to gloss over as mere cooperation or as a fair benefit for legal innocence.

In 2011 and again in 2018, I met with RW, who was an attorney in Oakland. RW had just finished a long string of stories about her work as a nonprofit attorney serving primarily Asian immigrant women in communities across San Francisco—communities in which she herself grew up. As we discussed the U visa, she shared her thoughts about both private practice and nonprofit legal work. "I mean, honestly, this is a criminal law issue. Women who are battered are protected by the criminal law system; people who are being trafficked are being protected by the criminal law system. How do you propose to stop or ameliorate it if you stop working with law enforcement agencies? Is there a way, can you think of any way? I can't."

RW's words revealed a sense of apprehension about what would happen if immigrant women were seen as anything other than legal subjects cooperating with law enforcement as crime victims. In my reading, her implicit meaning was that women who are battered are at the very least protected by the criminal legal system, and this protection, while insufficient in many ways, was the only path imaginable in our current moment. This limit of imagination is reinforced by the U visa.

In my conversations with legal advocates, there were many variations in how the usefulness and benefits of the visa were valued and critiqued. This specific political spectrum—a beginning marked at the entrance as *no other way* and reaffirmed at the exit as *only one way*—certainly elicited frustration on the part of legal advocates. As RW stated, "I mean, honestly, is there a way, can you think of a way? I can't." The apprehension RW expressed—"How do you propose to stop or ameliorate [violence] if you stop working with law enforcement agencies?"—runs through the life of the U visa and grounds the anxiety provoked by imagining the loss of visibility for women beyond this view. It also requires the continual disavowal of the relationship between policing and immigration. By narrating cooperation as freely given while at the same requiring it, the U visa forgets the conditions of violence already caused by immigration law. It disavows the fact that it is only by rendering undocumented immigrant women culpable in the first place that the law forces them to need the U visa, to fall beholden to an impossible condition where they must become part of enforcement to be protected, and, ultimately, to avoid their own punishment as well as the broader structures of punishment institutionalized against immigrant communities.

Thus, beyond attempts to classify the U visa as "good" or "bad" legislation, reflected in RW's question is the power of the visa to affect the death of political imagination. RW insightfully reflects on the fiction of nonconvergence, in which the law promises to distinguish between the innocence of the "good" immigrant, who survives not sexual violence per se but sexual violence as *crime*, and the culpability of the "bad" immigrant, who must be properly prosecutable for criminal activity. Without the presence of the *category* of a legal crime, and thus the racial difference and racial violence of criminalization and policing, there can be no protection. Further, survivors who face vulnerability due to their lack of legal status are *also* marked by law as "bad" immigrants for remaining without status—a position the law promises to remedy but instead only disavows. What I mean here is that the law's position of innocence for survivors imposes pressure for that innocence to be in its purest form in order to be exchangeable for U visa status. And the only pathway to this exchange is to be available for the purposes of policing. My concern, though, is that the biggest trick the law plays is to establish the liberal terms of protection as exceptional and to be valued by immigrant communities as a necessity and thus acceptable for our political futures. Instead, this legal fiction should be the analytical genesis for a radical critique of legal protection and punishment.

In contemporary immigration debates, cooperation is largely discussed as an agency-to-agency practice where local law enforcement has either agreed to cooperate with and provide information to federal immigration agencies, on the one hand, or has refrained from doing so, on the other. Contemporary sanctuary cities, ordinances, or state statutes are one example. In my fieldwork I found that cooperation with police played a profound role at a different level that manifested in the conditions antiviolence advocates had to navigate for their clients, the way they articulated and explained what it meant to cooperate, the way advocates understood themselves as members of Asian and Asian American communities, and the scope as well as limits of their work in people's lives. And so many of the ethnographic impasses I write about—differences between terms, unrecognizable commitments, and recognition of incommensurate pathways—foreground what unfolds when immigrant women are enlisted into serving policing's anti-Black logics in exchange for protection. It is about why, in our contemporary moment, it is so difficult to point to the violence of something like cooperation in modern US immigration law. It is also about the impasse that comes from immigrant women's experiences that *frustrate the law* because they both are used by the law to establish its terms of cooperation and, at the same time, are supposed to serve as the solution to the problems the law wishes to put forth. Put another way, VAWA's crime victim is the subject the law both targets to protect and uses to unfurl the racial logics of punishment—this dual bind marks the terms of cooperation and continues to rely on the development of a public notion of what crime is, what proper victimhood can be legible, and how criminality is understood through the racial logics of Blackness and criminality. Andrea Ritchie has argued that we need only look at the overpoliced and undersaved experiences of Black queer and trans survivors to register the ongoing violence of any legal reform effort that utilizes policing to achieve its goals.[32] This insight is profoundly important to understand what it means to navigate a legal protection for noncitizen survivors that is tied to overpolicing and undersaving.

In many ways, these political tensions I have discussed are not unfamiliar to Asian American studies paradigms that have long critiqued assimilationist agendas promoted by the nation-state. Here, Asian Americans framed as model-minority figures purportedly possessed inherent cultural behaviors and ethnic superiority that protected them and advanced them above racial others. As a historical discourse, the "model minority myth" describes the production of a racial narrative which misrepresents the category of Asian Americans to maintain white supremacy and anti-Black ideologies. Dylan Rodríguez argues that the myth cannot be understood outside its origins in militarized white reconstructionist laws and policies that created a sentimentality of security dependent on criminalization, whereby purported deviant racial categories were invented to establish who and what should be deemed as opposite the terms of security. Thus, the model minority myth emerged as a multicultural solution to the nation-state's "problem," which was not only blamed on Black bodies but reliant on the perpetual criminalization of racial and gendered categories.[33] In doing so, the celebration of Asian Americans as a model for all other communities hid the impact of neoliberal laws and policies that would result in forthcoming social and economic disparities. And even further, it transferred into the neoliberal responsibility narratives used by social welfare and policing agencies as well. Not only was it a myth that Asians did not experience hardship, but it was a legal fiction that Asianness would somehow transfer from one racial subject to another and bootstrap others upward.

Under the U visa scheme, cooperation functions as a literal assimilationist act. The requirement for legal certification is the determining factor as to whether a survivor can remain or even be eligible to assimilate to begin with. Further, the figure of the cooperator establishes the promise of mobility away from violence and hardship, which is synonymous with the model minority myth but also extends beyond it. For while the paradigm of this myth hinges on the position of Asians against other communities marked as racial problems, the figure of the cooperator not only promises to deal with other "bad immigrants" by policing them but purportedly corrects itself by promising to temporarily remove a survivor's undocumented condition. The undocumented crime victim as a legal subject reproduces the racial figure of the assimilationist "good" immigrant. We must refuse the making of survivors into cooperators because this legal subject reifies the dichotomy of the model minority myth's "good" versus "bad" immigrant divide.[34] Most insightfully, Pooja Gehi and Soniya Munshi have argued that Asian American political and scholarly critique of the racial logic of a model race for liberal reform should extend to the racial violence of criminalization.[35] Here, Gehi and Munshi show that the model minority myth both produces and reinforces hierarchies within Asian American categories that are further entrenched by what they identify as the *model-minority victim* as a systemic effect of the political landscape that unfolds through neoliberal policy reform coupled with VAWA. Thus, under the U visa, the law creates a bind between each legal figure and the racial violence attached to the promise of protection. In my reading, a semipermanent racial tension stands within attempts to establish any critique of legal protection coupled with the fleeting possibility of a kind of protection that can only ever be temporary.

Conclusion

Most of my thinking for this book came from my time during graduate school and fieldwork between Michigan and California. But long before I conducted interviews for this book or even entered graduate studies, I spent several years working with Asian American and multiracial coalitional organizations across Los Angeles and Southern California. Some of this work came from community-based collective organizing efforts, but the majority of my time went to varying short-term jobs with different nonprofits. At one of these jobs, I worked at an Asian American legal center, which found itself faced with the question of whether the organization would sign on to a coalition letter to reform crack cocaine sentencing laws to reduce their racial targeting of Black spaces. At the time, several of us attempted to push the organization to sign and align with political critiques of sentencing laws. In the end, the organization did not sign the letter, citing a purported need to respect and adhere to our clients, who were "victims of crimes, not people who committed crimes."

In many ways, this event shaped my political commitments and intellectual challenges in the years to follow. I was unaware of this at the time, but the victim, as a subject of legal meaning making, would come to occupy my exploration into the workings of race, gender, and the law as well as the ideologies and political practices that emerge as paradigmatic immigrant rights narratives. While racial analysis of victims has many markers, I am interested in a slightly different vein—victimhood as the imposed frame on which feminist of color thought is often most registered as acceptable and legible. For me, the theoretical insights and political practices that created ways of addressing gender-based violence without ignoring race have always had to push off the dominance of victim-based frameworks in liberal discourses and state apparatuses. In law, this particular set of approaches highlights the need to interrogate the attachment between protection and punishment in law, which is often rendered as a practical necessity, productive and useful. What I hope this chapter can provide is a reorientation away from that attachment and the specific mythology of protection as a singular policy solution purportedly disconnected from racial violence. Instead, I suggest that any making of the victim as a legal figure is always and already encompassed by the productive relationship between protection and punishment guarded by political terms of practicality and necessity. To open critique of the legal subject of the crime victim without completely disregarding or reifying the material legal practices tied to what survivors need, we might interrogate the racial meaning making produced by the actual design of a specific law and the practices that ensue from it.

Currently, most political debates continue to invoke rape as a linchpin through which police violence, immigration violence, and the violence of prisons are postponed, rather than talking about harm in ways that put resources into community-driven housing, health, and mental health in non-punitive ways often reproduced by program management from within the nonprofit industrial complex and its reliance on federal and state funding. Often, immigrant survivors are painted as *too* fearful and unwilling to come forward and cooperate with police prosecutions. Survivors are expected to fulfill an impossible expectation to improve safety for the public overall, save their own lives, end any fear of police, and improve police functions. It is curious that the most vulnerable, those with the least resources, are made to be responsible for the betterment of everyone's safety. Undocumented survivors are weaponized to humanize the violence of policing and legitimate its role in safety. Yet, continually, the policing structure and immigration system through which many undocumented communities come in contact with the law to begin with are in effect more justified, more humanized, and rendered as more nonviolent by the U visa scheme— *immigration law is violent, but protections are an exception.*

The U visa's certification requirement and the demand for cooperation must end. Until then, no matter how willing a law enforcement agent is or how quickly a certification is signed, the weaponization of survivor vulnerability continues. But still, even with the unforeseeable possibility that something like cooperation will be lifted, a different kind of political imagining and relationality must continue to be built among communities that live with violence and seek accountability from harm. This is why abolition feminist thinking is imperative as a community organizing practice, way of writing, and a means of thinking through the violence of protection.

I hope this chapter has provided a way to critique the expectations set by U visa law without either submerging analysis under the domain of practicality and necessity or shoring up the materiality at the level of reform. At the center of an approach toward a critical discussion of the legal figure of the undocumented crime victim is the racial assemblage of cooperation and mutual exchange as legal designs and discourses through which victimhood is produced and maintained. It is only through attention to this terrain that we can examine the relationship between protection and punishment and the reach of the victim subject. We must turn to abolition feminist thought and lives to work away from the liberal genre of protection that enforces the legal fiction of mutual exchange and the racial logics of criminalization. Without this, we reproduce the terms of law and foreclose futures for survivors to the limit of what is correctable by law.

3

The Contractable Victim

THE RACIAL FIGURE OF THE
MODERN-DAY SLAVE, INJURY, AND SURVEILLANCE
IN ANTITRAFFICKING LAW

"I'm an attorney, so ultimately, I'm trying to help my clients get some kind of temporary or permanent status so they won't be deported. But my goal is *also* this—to skip the number of times they have to tell their story." In the San Francisco Bay Area, BW was an attorney who worked for many years in Asian American immigrant rights and had recently joined a network of social workers, attorneys, and case managers focused on trafficking across the Bay Area. For BW, reducing the amount of contact with immigration agents a client had to endure was an important legal strategy, and this came up frequently in our conversations. The advocacy goal wasn't simply to reduce her client's contact with enforcement agencies, but the *story*. Even if a survivor's story resulted in a legal success, there was an uneasiness and a risk that BW often referenced regardless of whether a story resulted in both failed and successful cases. As part of the much broader history of trafficking's gendered global and political economies, advocates like BW worked in a very particular site of law where undocumented survivors already residing within the borders of the nation-state may be eligible to be legal subjects as *crime victims* and receive protection in the form of temporary legal status. In previous chapters I discussed legal protections under the Violence Against Women Act (VAWA) and the racial and gendered conditions of cooperation the law expects from survivors and the terms of protection tied to policing. What is the difference between experiences that successfully meet the law's expectations and those that can never qualify? BW's brief articulation pushes us to pause and think through the legal figure anchored by law's design.

Stemming from the late 1990s and early 2000s, United Nations conventions and protocols to advance the international "fight to end human trafficking" originate priorities of nation-state security regimes and border regulation rather than centering the lives of migrants, women, or girls despite the signification of their bodies. Women of color feminist critiques of such antitrafficking campaigns have argued that the structural violence of human trafficking does not begin or end with "bad actors" but rather with the global political economy, militarized humanitarianism, the feminized labor of racial capitalism, nation-state international agreements on peace and war, and ongoing projects of imperialism and settler colonialism.[1] Transnational feminist scholars have advanced racial and gendered critiques of Western feminist antitrafficking discourses tied to the 2000 Victims of Trafficking and Violence Protection Act and the United Nations Convention on Transnational Crime. Kamala Kempadoo has emphasized how "moral panics" over women's sexuality and domestic heteronormativity bolstered security regimes and immigration control against developing nations under antitrafficking campaigns.[2] Tracing to geopolitics of the 1990s when international law first defined sexual violence as a war crime against humanity, Rana Jaleel's work has shown how this post–Cold War era of US empire instilled the naming of rape to abstract social differences and produce racial, colonial, and imperial orders.[3] Laura Kang has argued that the category of Asian woman throughout post–Cold War politics was particularly *portable* and served to be demonstrative of sexual violation that fit the interests of Western international human rights recourse. This led to the submersion of other intra-Asian violences invested in militarized strategies of sexual violence and control and the suppression of transnational feminist and global political movements to address labor exploitation and war.[4] Jennifer Suchland's insights have shown that postsocialist geopolitics and prosecutorial responses to "violence against women" condition how trafficking is studied and addressed today through the racial meaning of colorblindness, which relies on the legal and political identification of the victim of "violence against women" and the "loser of globalization."[5]

In this chapter I focus on the violence of legal protection within T nonimmigrant status, legislated in 2000 under the Trafficking Victims Protection Act (TVPA), passed as part of the US Victims of Trafficking and Violence Protection Act. T nonimmigrant status is commonly referred to as the "T visa," but it does not function like a typical visa application process for those outside a nation-state to then enter. The T visa was designed specifically to provide legal status for survivors of "severe forms" of human trafficking who already reside within the nation-state but do not have legal status or are at risk of losing their status.[6] I will refer to the "T visa" and "T legal status" interchangeably. T nonimmigrant status does not necessarily or automatically lead to any pathway to permanency within the United States, and "severe form of human trafficking" is defined as including both sex trafficking and labor trafficking.[7] At the time of this book's writing, T status is a four-year temporary status available to those who qualify as crime victims; are physically present (in the United States, American Samoa, or the Northern Mariana Islands, or at a port of entry); have complied with a request to assist law enforcement in the "detection, investigation, or prosecution of human trafficking"; can demonstrate that they would experience extreme hardship if removed from the United States; and have evidence that they are admissible to the US or are applying for a waiver of inadmissibility.[8] Under certain conditions, some family members may be eligible to apply for T nonimmigrant status and apply for work authorization if they are present in the United States or after they arrive in the United States but must be lawfully admitted. T status holders receive authorization for employment and become eligible to adjust their status to lawful permanent residency (green card) after three years of living continuously in the United States with T status. There is an incentive to assist with law enforcement: If T nonimmigrant visa holders are physically present while assisting a US investigation and prosecution of criminalized activity—specifically, trafficking—they do not have to wait three years to become eligible for permanent residency.[9] Some are eligible to receive some health and welfare benefits on certification of a bona fide approval of T status (also available to those who are granted continued presence as qualifying victims and potential witnesses in prosecution).[10] The T visa is capped at five thousand per year (not including derivative status granted to family members).[11]

Dominant antitrafficking discourses are less reflective of the actual lives of trafficked persons and more reflective of state power as a rescuer. I am primarily concerned with the relationship between racial surveillance and policing anchored to the T visa. What is the racial figure and the legal subject of the T visa against the structural geopolitical conditions tied to "antitrafficking," and what other questions are pertinent for feminist of color critiques of the problem and the solutions produced through T visa law? I engage insights from attorneys and case managers from Asian American serving organizations; some were critical of surveillance and criminalization, and some were less so. Because federal immigration and local enforcement agencies also carry out antitrafficking programs to "protect borders" and "fight crime," ethnographic material in this chapter centers not only on how the T visa application unfolds but also on the racial and gendered politics between advocates and law enforcement and between advocates and their clients.[12] For advocates like BW, cooperation was not merely at the level of an individual case, but through institutionally funded relationships like assisting after an immigration raid, coauthoring reports, or merely having to maintain a relationship that already impacted current clients. Following the larger argument put forward in this book, the "undocumented crime victim" is not a person but a legal subject that survivors must become eligible *as* to then apply for protections and undergo some kind of exchange.

"I still think this is a good law," BW emphasized; I heard this interpretation frequently throughout my fieldwork, and this posed a challenge for my ethnographic writing. In particular, how do we write about the violence of law when it is doing something "good" or when someone's lived experience does not sufficiently provide evidence of a "bad" law's impact? In many ways, these difficulties are often at the center of political movements for communities of color, care practices, and advocacy efforts that work to address harm while also critiquing solutions that either do not serve them or serve them only when they are of a certain value. We might see this exemplification in the racial figure of the "modern-day slave" tied to antitrafficking discourses. The modern-day slave is a dominant frame through which the legal subject of victim is tied to crime and maintained under the T visa scheme.

Many of the legal advocates I spoke with struggled with their criticisms of antitrafficking law. A survivor who received a T visa could mean the difference between being placed into deportation proceedings or not. But like the previous chapters of this book have argued, this difference is racially assembled and not without expectation, burden, and violence that require our political and intellectual theories of refusals and reorientations. The interpretations advocates articulated, their relationships with their clients, and tensions between and within antitrafficking networks and immigrant rights coalitions are all conditions that reflect what I view as central to discourses produced by the law. The T visa legal subject is simultaneously expected to reflect a policing agenda, women's rescue, state security, international humanitarianism, border security and much more. With all of these conditions placed upon survivors who attempt to be legible as T visa "crime victims," it is no wonder that other tensions are produced for applicants and for advocates. Thus, in this chapter I consider how the racial figure of the modern-day slave produces a non-Black legal subject whose cooperation is harnessed to aid in anti-immigrant state projects of security and policing under antitrafficking law. The advocacy efforts presented in this chapter reflect the T visa legal scheme as a site where the racial logics of criminalization and international security and surveillance agendas continue to be entangled under the promise of legal protection waged against the vulnerabilities immigrant survivors undergo.

The Contractable Victim

In San Francisco I met several times with CL to speak about legal advocacy and trafficking.[13] When she first started practicing law, her focus was always on Asian American communities, and most of the policy and legal issues were focused on immigration, citizenship, and housing. This was a period she described as "before" government agencies became interested in funding issues related to trafficking. Several large cases in the Bay Area came to light involving Indian women and girls who had been sponsored to the United States, labored in small businesses owned by the men who recruited them, and were expected to be sexual companions. There were several deaths, and the exploitation of labor and immigration were brought to light as cases of labor and sex trafficking. At the time, CL and her colleagues from legal nonprofits and women's shelters provided language translation, access to shelters and temporary housing, mental health services, and food and continued to do that work on their own, eventually searching for federal and state funding to establish trafficking as one of the policy areas her organization would agree to address. "I had to convince everyone," she shared. I asked why, and CL responded that despite some media attention in the Bay Area, "I had to convince the rest of the staff that this was an Asian American legal issue area." During the Bush presidential administration in the early 2000s, federal funds tied to broader militarized humanitarian agendas became available specifically for antitrafficking legal and social services available to local nonprofit organizations. CL shared that several nonprofits applied for or were awarded these funds that were driven by the administration's political agenda of establishing moral goals and religious values within federally funded programs. The most dominant political voices that drove antitrafficking politics were mostly white, religious Western-based NGOs without any prior interest in substantive immigrant rights or larger Asian American or diasporic community issues, despite their interest on women from Asia. CL shared:

> CL: The fight against modern-day slavery fit with the right-wing, conservative Christian coalition model of rescuing people. It fit for the Bush administration's agendas, so the funding also came with gag provisions. You couldn't advise clients on family planning or abortion, for example, if you received federal funding.... So there are these ties, to federal funds, that really reflect, I think, the political perspective of the religious right, that really jumped on this human trafficking issue.... One of the most challenging obstacles [we faced in antitrafficking work] was that there were these major groups, anti-prostitution versus legalization/sex workers rights. And these two groups totally butt heads; they conflated prostitution with sex trafficking, you know, it was like, you were either for ending slavery or you were a supporter of sex workers....

> INTERVIEWER: These were mostly white [organizations]?

> CL: Yes. And we stayed out of it; our position has always been ... we don't care and we don't pass judgment about what choices or industries they have worked in or participated in. Our concern is, are you a survivor, do you need help, and how do we help you, and that's it.

Elizabeth Bernstein has shown that even competing "feminist gender equality" and Christian evangelical groups that claim to align under proclaimed shared interests tied to human trafficking continue to promote the violence of militarized humanitarianisms and ideologies of carceral punishment against bodies that threaten heteronormative political agendas tied to gender and sexuality.[14] Elena Shih has further demonstrated how international rescue campaigns concerned with human trafficking reproduce additional harms against the women who serve as objects of this rescue and disavow concerns over the reification of exploitative labor while seemingly saving women from forced labor.[15] Contemporary antitrafficking projects that cross borders continue to exemplify the violence of Western humanitarian savior campaigns to rescue "Other" women, invent the need to save women from their own culture—often to redeem the culture and supremacy of the West. Religious groups and international aid campaigns not only generate a nonprofit industrial complex supported by nation-state agreements and funding pipelines but also invoke the figure of woman-as-victim when designing and implementing policy solutions, educational programs, cultural exchanges, and microbusinesses that purport to liberate women by focusing on traffickers as bad actors. Yet such campaigns are often unwilling to shift, critique, or eradicate the conditions of imperialism, racial capitalism, settler colonialism, and genocide to begin with.

Over several years, CL's organization and their partners began to receive calls from individuals inquiring about services related to human trafficking. From there, they decided to build a more systematized set of legal services and formal partnerships with social work case managers. Law enforcement agencies also began calling. CL shared, "They know to call one of us now." For CL, there was a clear break from the time *before* this shift in federal funding, and I asked what would typically have happened to someone if they were held because of an immigration raid on a workplace or a residence before that shift. Before the introduction of T status and other provisions for undocumented survivors in 2000, CL's organization mostly relied on VAWA benefits for immigration relief. However, these were available only to survivors who had existing legal status tied to a US citizen or legal permanent resident who had sponsored them. Applying for asylum was also available only to those who had remained in the nation-state for less than a year. But most important, CL emphasized, "All of this was contingent on even finding out, figuring out, [that you are] eligible for immigration relief... and then you somehow have to find an attorney... so I have to assume most women were deported."

As advocacy for survivors grew, so did an encroaching relationship with both federal immigration and law enforcement agencies. In the interviews I conducted, every advocate expressed hesitancy; some interpreted the hesitancy as less significant compared to the benefit, others questioned the long-term implications for Asian American and multiracial antipolice and prison abolition coalitions, and yet others expressed that their personal reflections did not matter because in their professional practice they had no other choice. CL summarized these interpretations in this way:

> I understand I have to walk this fine line between cooperating and standing firm. [We] cannot just obey.... That's not going to work out for [our] communities. If someone tells you, do this or that, our general response is to ask, Why? and Is this the right thing to do? I think if we are protecting [a client's] interest, you have a responsibility for them.... So not just jumping when government says to jump... and I've tried to establish a working relationship with federal and state law enforcement that understands that... we aren't just going to roll over for them.... We've had to earn a reputation... as zealous advocates but being respectful and easy to work with.

While CL spoke plainly about this condition of being zealous but respectful and easy at the same time, the extremity of this pressure was significant to me because I heard it repeatedly from others in slightly different ways.

Later, as we talked about a challenging case, this tension emerged again—but this time not only in the advocate's practice but in the survivor's as well. CL was working on a T visa application. Her client was a survivor, a sex worker in the Bay Area, and was referred to CL from another organization that had provided social welfare resources. If the T application was successful, she could avoid deportation and be eligible for work authorization and remain in the San Francisco Bay Area. When reflecting on Asian American legal advocacy for survivors, CL shared that there were two main components, immigration and gender, where the former was clear-cut with a delineated end, but the latter was ongoing:

> There are so many clients, you can help them with immigration visas, so they can work lawfully, getting assistance with housing, so their material needs are met. But the thing that made them vulnerable in the first place, which is tied to gender . . . What is their understanding of that? One huge example . . . [my] client, we went into a law enforcement interview, and the US attorney and FBI agents are asking her questions, all white men, and she is giggling . . . downplaying a lot of the harm that happened to her. And so I ask for a moment to talk to her in private, and I ask her why she is doing this. I'm telling her that this is not the time to downplay what happened to her, what she told me was very different than what she was saying [in the interview]. And she says, "Well, they [FBI] are the ones that have the power, and I have a feeling that the more innocent and clean I am, the more they will want to help me."

This is the story of someone going *against* the advice of her attorney. CL's client knew very little about the American legal system or the details of the T visa for that matter, but her sense of how law enforcement viewed her and what the law expected pushed her to silence her own experience and her own words.

In the interview room, CL's client was responding to a source of force imposed by the law enforcement agent and by the legal subject she was attempting to be positioned through: a crime victim. She sought to be *more* innocent and *more* clean—so that "they" (white men) would want to help her. But CL's client also knew that she had to meet the expectation that she could help law enforcement as well, with a willingness to assist with prosecution. She needed to be more innocent and more clean, not to be saved or rescued, but to be *contractable* and to cooperate in a useful way with law enforcement's antitrafficking agendas. In this moment, enforcement's antitrafficking agendas and nonprofit advocacy agendas are supposed to align. As CL continued, she discussed her client's racial and gendered migration as a survivor of sex trafficking and as an undocumented Asian woman—conditions of harm and vulnerability. At the same time, performing sex work and remaining in the United States without legal status were also conditions that American laws criminalized, and while being a crime victim was a legal subject position that promised to remove culpability, on some level CL's client questioned whether being a crime victim would make her innocent and clean *enough*. CL did not share whether this client received the T visa. Immediately after discussing this application, she discussed the case of another client who successfully applied for T status. With this second application, CL wondered, "In the end, ... what I think is the most frustrating is that you don't know, at the end of this, whether or not they felt this was their choice, whether they are free to make choices."

I took field notes immediately after this conversation, and my original notes recorded both clients as examples of unsuccessful cases. In this moment, they read to me as experiences where both clients endured violent endings, even though one client received the T visa and the other's legal outcome was unknown. Regardless of the outcome, the broader workings of law placed survivors in conditions where they had to match their lived experiences to racial figures in order to become eligible to stand as legal subjects. And this matching—whether through the telling or erasing of one's own words—reflected the workings of the T visa schema. Although it was not CL's intention to describe different scenarios, her extended reflection about what was most frustrating "in the end" highlighted a reference to freedom, what that would look like and whether advocacy efforts hindered or advanced this possibility. With this reflection, CL spoke not only as an attorney but also as a member of multiple political and social communities working for women, for Asian Americans, for sex workers, for immigrants.

Wendy Brown has argued that "politicized identity politics" cling to wounded attachments and willingly rely on injury to establish rights-based claims that neither lead to emancipated freedoms nor eradicate the consuming force of Western humanity's universalisms on minoritized groups.[16] Brown argues that politicized identities desire to establish only their suffering and pain, through which they gain freedom by repeating only the wound of what "I am" rather than the freedoms of what "I want." Brown focuses heavily on "feminist politics" to exemplify this critique; under this formulation the pursuit of legal protection falls beholden to the masculinist delivery of political rights, entrenches Western liberalism, and orients itself only through revenge against injury, thereby hindering politicized identities from achieving political freedom.

While I am also concerned about the liberal politics of seeking state protection, I am focused on the racial assemblage of law that makes such protection successful and available to some and not others, and the terms on which that success depends. I depart from the argument that frames such pursuits of protection as injurious desire lodged in politicized identities, as Brown argues. My departure is based on racial violence and a distinction of legal protection; immigrant survivors who navigate the crime victim subject do so not because they desire to be recognized as injured, but because of the conditions the law has imposed upon them toward deportation and punishment. They can never fully become a solely injured subject let alone speak as one that desires that injury because "victim" is already bound to other things; it is both the object of protection and the subject that unfurls punishment. As for the dominance of white feminist antiviolence politics I reference in this book, its wound of the injured "I am" is in part only possible because of the larger placement of what "they are" onto racial others. And through this, the political voice that attempts to achieve state recognition as an injurious subject is rooted in whiteness as political violence that promotes a neutral stance toward policing, criminalization, and immigration enforcement to "save women."

A wounded attachment is a white attachment, and my point is not to excuse any existing Asian American contemporary politics that attempt to emulate this frame or engage in political alliances with white injured womanhood. If anything, I am talking back to these political positions. And while I agree that injury-based political recognition from the state requires critique, the problem for me is not that the politicized identity misplaces freedom but that the law's demand for victimhood is enforced upon minoritized groups. For example, I take issue with the fact that immigrants are occasionally protected. It is the law's particular enforcement of punishment in exchange for protection that unfurls the ideological tensions among antitrafficking, immigrant rights, victim rights, and abolition feminist political movements. It is not that Asian American survivors choose to speak only through wounded attachments but that a larger racial discourse of punishment established policing as the basis for legal remedies and these remedies are *enforced*. The enforcement secures the victim as a legal subject position from which minoritized groups must grapple with several conditions—the difficulty of becoming an object of proper victimhood and the expectation to already be willing subjects of policing. Alexander Weheliye has argued that the problem Brown identifies is not so much a minority subject's desire to "cling to his or her pain but a consequence of the dogged insistence on suffering as the only price of entry to proper personhood."[17] Survivors, for example, do not speak "I am" but rather are enforced into a constant shuttling between innocence and culpability, victim and cooperator. Last, legal protections are not merely isolated but rather already entrenched in the bind to another site of the political—legal punishment via a racial assemblage, the most troubling aspect of which results in the criminalization of the harmed person or coerced cooperation. In other words, the universal victim may be reified in Brown's formulation unless the racial assemblage of what sits opposite the proper injury is theorized and accounted for. Thus, in my view, the problem with legal protection is that it racially assembles the violence of punishment through which the promise of freedom is temporary and *enforced*. While a host of contemporary political voices everywhere do indeed reproduce the wounded attachments and troubling white feminist frameworks of liberal rights, we must distinguish between the misguided apprehension of freedom and the legal legibility that suppresses suffering.

The Modern-Day Slave and the Good/Bad Immigrant Paradigm

The Trafficking Victims Protection Act (TVPA) focuses on three specific areas: methods of legal relief, prevention, and enforcement within the borders of the United States and internationally. In this way, the law's trajectory is commonly presented as a progression from prior limited and failed efforts to address human trafficking that left survivors to remain in detention, for their lack of legal status. This authorized the Department of Justice to administer trafficking victims services funds to grantees across multiple states, $90 million in appropriations funding to DOJ for victim services, additional funds come from the Domestic Trafficking Victims' Fund support existing grants, and Health and Human Services Office on Trafficking Persons administers victim services grants as well.[18] Julie Dahlstrom has argued that administrative policies actively play a role in hindering approvals of T visa applications.[19] USCIS policies have increased burdens on T visa applicants, such as placing a denied applicant into immediate deportation removal proceedings, restricting standards for approved fee waiver requests, raising fees, and summarily rejecting applications due to filing errors or noncompliance with fees.[20] Further, while more TVPA funds were allocated to the Department of Health and Human Services through the development of a new Crime Victim Justice Corps, and more undocumented persons have been categorized as potentially eligible to apply for T status, the maximum number of T visas made available per year is never reached.[21] Additionally troubling, TVPA funds do not go to community care, advocacy, and service providers—where the funds could have a direct impact for survivors—unless they are largely tied to nonprofit and governmental partnerships related to "modern-day slavery" and some form of immigration enforcement or security agenda.

Jennifer Chacón argues that congressional antitrafficking legislation that centers around the inclusion of migrants and those laws that orient toward the enforcement against migrant entry are often overlapping and contradictory in their legal provisions and proposed policy solutions.[22] Sarah Deer and Sarah Hunt have separately argued that antitrafficking legislation and political campaigns locate economic systems as global and abroad, always emphasizing the crossing of nation-state borders.[23] This, in turn, discounts Indigenous lands and people, on which borders are imposed rather than crossed. Legislative efforts continually promise to distinguish between trafficked and nontrafficked movement but through the specific formulation of targeting only a certain kind of movement—coerced, forced, and fraudulent—across borders, while still policing the border itself, regardless of movement, in the name of saving trafficked women, surveillance, and enforcement.[24] As Annie Hill has demonstrated about the rhetoric of modern-day slavery, antitrafficking is a peculiar and particular set of global enactments that should be read synonymously with anti-immigrant legislation and xenophobic state agendas.[25]

Following Hill's insights, the T visa's antitrafficking agenda is a tandem trajectory of enforcement alongside the pro-policing politics of mainstream campaigns seeking to end violence against women. The TVPA's securitization of borders set the stage for the T visa's rescue, which is reliant on the sign of woman not as the object of policing per se but as policing itself. In this way, the vulnerability of survivors must remain solidified, unchanging, and pure in its form of innocence—to remain eligible to receive the solution (protection) while still producing value for the primary purpose of enforcement. "Antitrafficking" solutions such as the T visa are in many ways permanently unfulfilled regardless of policy improvements or the behaviors of bad actors, not because the law is contradictory in its promise, but because of its original design.

Antitrafficking law does not produce protection and punishment as detached mechanisms of law but binds them through the making of a singular position of the legal subject of the victim, racially assembled through the figure of the modern-day slave. While it is appealing to argue that antitrafficking laws have progressed to establish more inclusive varieties of what constitutes the victim subject, this progress-based narrative is deeply misguided and disavows the existing reliances on racialized punishment that hinges on the vulnerability of survivors. Further, even while adherence to the position of victim is a necessary legal position one must occupy in order to qualify for benefits or legal relief, the necessity of appealing to the modern-day slave to make survivors' legally legible relies on an unavoidable racial figure and expectation. Why *modern-day slave*? One advocate I spoke with suggested that victimized images and narratives could provide some immediate benefit to a client but asked, "But in the long term, I don't know, does that help communities?"

TP was an attorney who had assisted with several T visa applications. We spoke about the discourse of modern-day slavery. To be a victim according to the TVPA's definition of "severe forms of human trafficking," evidence of coercion, such as labor against one's own will, had to be present. TP's clients had to show force, either physical or psychological, or through deception. "There was a case that involved several women; they weren't physically forced with locks or handcuffs or anything like that. They could move throughout the home and walk in and out of doors. They signed contracts with the trafficker to pay off debt, and they weren't planning to try to return home until that debt was paid. During law enforcement interviews, the interviewers kept asking, 'Why didn't you leave? You had a key to the door. Why didn't you just leave?'"

TP and I spoke several times about this advocacy effort and the reference to leaving or staying not only in law enforcement interviews but also within the overall T status scheme. Whether migration would constitute a sufficiently severe form of human trafficking hinged on leaving, staying, coming, and going, often referencing and relying on perceptions of the figure of the modern-day slave. How do we think through a condition where to be protected by the law, one must successfully become a modern-day slave? Some of TP's clients endured severe migration but not severe trafficking; they were not eligible for resources or protection. TP shared, "In a weird way, the T visa scheme . . . is almost only for those people that really want to stay here. But many originally came with the intent of making money and then going home, but if you want legal relief, that's not an option. [The law] says you either stay or you leave permanently."

In antitrafficking law, there is indeed a "perfect victim," and that perfect victim is the figure of the modern-day slave. If the geopolitical conditions of trafficking constitute structures of violence at hand far beyond the mere individuality of traffickers, and if the borders imposed and crossed are reinforced by antitrafficking legislation that enforces, surveils, and punishes, then the T visa scheme not only produces the perfect victim of the modern-day slave but positions this legal subject to be part of a security and policing apparatus. There is a material relationship between legal practice and the written letter of law. There is also a discursive and temporal condition to legal meaning making in how a law is understood by some, explained to others, and even politicized. It is here that one component of the racial and gendered logics of law is exemplified in the legal figures produced by a legal rule, regulation, and statute.[26] The advocacy stories shared in this chapter exemplify different scenarios where a survivor downplays victimhood, a story is held back, or the physical presence is rendered as not enough. Thus, the violence we might see imposed on T visa applications is not merely the impossibility of becoming perfect victims ("innocent and clean" for CL's client) but also the burden of expectation referenced through the modern-day slave to animate the contractability of the crime victim. The violence of this contractability is its propensity to aid in law enforcement's antitrafficking campaigns, designed to help the *part* of a survivor who is a legal victim but punish the *other part* who is an unauthorized migrant who does not correctly decide to "leave" or "stay" (TP's client). This legal fracturing imposed on survivors breaks in order to advance the primary agenda of border security and surveillance under the liberal politics of rescuing and restoring victims.

In a congressional hearing on "The Global Fight to End Modern Day Slavery," the US Committee on Foreign Relations heard testimony urging lawmakers to broaden "modern-day slavery" to cover "severe forms of labor exploitation that exist today" where, "instead of shackles and chains, workers are now enslaved through threats, debt and other forms of economic coercion."[27] The hearing emphasized the reframing of slavery as the exploitation of workers and wage earners primarily from the "Middle East, Southeast Asia, India, African nation-states, and the Pacific" as a distinct turn away from discussions of colonization, imperialism, genocide, or militarization continuing into the present. Speakers from international nongovernmental organizations funded by Western nation-states drew data from a US-created index measuring rates of trafficking in other countries. The higher the trafficking rate, the harsher the proposed US economic sanctions would be imposed on that country or nation-state.[28]

Elizabeth Bernstein has traced the political formation of modern-day slavery in its inconsistencies across law, nongovernmental organizations, and state agencies, none of which have ever been transparent about the definition of modern-day slavery or its usages.[29] If current antitrafficking legislation defines "severe forms of human trafficking" based on the severity of coercion, injury, and violation of labor and sex, why invoke slavery in particular, and what renders it "modern"? Lyndsey Beutin has argued that antitrafficking narratives stem from modernity's European civilizational missions that establish a global racial order. The "modern" campaign is exemplified in media productions that circulate and visualize modern-day slavery through repeated invocations of Blackness yet do so only to produce white indemnity and the promise of a white abolition.[30] Robyn Maynard has shown that North American antitrafficking campaigns are able to rely on references to modern-day slavery because of the denial of Black suffering within these political discourses, which "whitewashes" the conditions faced by Black sex workers, who form the majority of those criminalized for sex work, whether trafficked or not.[31] Maynard emphasizes that the absence of Black suffering in existing antitrafficking political discourses is even more troubling when placed alongside the overpresence of Blackness as the target of policing and criminal enforcement. These insights taken together highlight the absence of federal-wide protections for sex workers, who are eligible for protection only if successfully transposed into the legal definition of severe forms of human trafficking couched in whiteness and modern-day slavery.

Tiffany Lethabo King writes, "The infinite possibilities for fungible Black flesh mark a fundamental distinction between fungible slave bodies and non-Black (exploited) laboring bodies."[32] King argues that labor is a discursive site on which law incorporates and includes non-Black bodies to become constitutive of the liberal state. In doing so, labor sets the terms on which liberal claims constitute the non-Black subject, or the subject that can never incorporate Blackness—the laborer, the worker. Legal protections such as the T visa formulate labor trafficking to also produce terms of belonging (the leaving and staying) bound to a structure of erasure. We might consider the political discourse of the modern-day slave to be constitutive of the liberal genre of the human through this very conflation of slavery as labor exploitation. In this way, "modern-day slavery" reduces Black captivity to the exploitation of work, on the one hand, and produces a non-Black legal subject (crime victim) whose cooperation is harnessed to aid in state agendas of security and border enforcement, on the other.

Labor conditions, work sites, and transportation for migrants are already highly targeted by immigration enforcement agencies that detain and deport migrant workers. If the discourse surrounding the "modern-day slave" promises to highlight labor exploitation for the benefit of trafficked persons, it is curious that such discourses say nothing to critique anti-immigrant laws that instill surveillance, detention, and deportation of migrant communities. This is in part because antitrafficking discourses rely so heavily on the paradigm of the good/bad immigrant that promises to expel "bad" immigrants and retain the "good." Yet, as much of this book has discussed, Asian American Studies and Ethnic Studies scholarship has long argued that such paradigms are examples of Western imperialisms that function both domestically and globally to embolden state power through false racial tropes that fuel racial profiling, policing, and surveillance. While antitrafficking laws promise to benefit only the survivor or the good immigrant, the law's design relies completely on always maintaining the paradigm of the good/bad rather than dismantling it. Thus, antitrafficking laws are often less about the survivor-as-rescued and more reflective of the state-as-rescuer.

The Raid and the Rescue

The TVPA funded the Rescue and Restore Program under the Department of Health and Human Services in 2004. Approximately $2.2 million was made available to fund nearly a dozen grants to build antitrafficking efforts through the Anti-Trafficking in Persons Programs. These programs established Rescue and Restore coalitions among nonprofits, law enforcement, and researchers across twenty-four cities and states.[33] The Rescue and Restore grant application described the program as a "cooperative agreement" to spread public information about human trafficking and increase the identification of individuals perceived to be trafficked. Organizations receiving grants were intended to serve as regional "focal points," conduct outreach, and identify those who may be eligible to be crime victims. As part of regional programs, they were expected to function with law enforcement and carried the responsibility to encourage a broader localized cooperative structure.[34] However, when it came to T visa applications, all of the attorneys and case managers I spoke with shared that an overwhelming majority of trafficking clients did not walk through the front doors of their offices but rather were referred through law enforcement first. It is not surprising that most survivors, sex workers, or undocumented persons face barriers to knowledge of and access to the legal system. But it is alarming that some end up being more likely (and in some cases exceptionally so) to come in contact with legal and social services because of a referral by law enforcement agencies. That a partnership must exist for that contact to occur is notable, particularly when one side of this partnership is actively involved in the policing and punishment of sexuality and race and in doing so yields power over the other. We might imagine all the other ways outreach and recruitment could take place if cooperating with police was not so heavily funded and if the mechanism of policing was not attached to this legal protection couched in the campaign to end "modern-day slavery."

Because of its primary purpose, Rescue and Restore was based on an alliance through a variety of partnerships—law enforcement, social service, faith-based groups, immigrant outreach programs, health care, and legal assistance. Second, Rescue and Restore emphasized public awareness about the specificities of sex and labor trafficking. At TVPA hearings, the Administration for Children and Families' principal deputy assistant secretary, Christopher Gersten, described the program as a campaign "designed to overcome the barriers the federal government has experienced in identifying and rescuing victims—barriers that keep victims well-hidden from society's view even as they live among us." The testimony emphasized Rescue and Restore's focus on improving law enforcement and encouraging the public's participation.[35] The deputy assistant secretary's testimony continued to emphasize the program's assistance in the enforcement of law and the public's assistance in policing "victims hidden in plain sight."[36]

"Public awareness" itself invites anyone to partake in the public identification of potential victims. The invitation to enhance a general gaze *on hidden victims* is a call to identify who and what sounds and acts like a victim. The call to gaze is not derived from an actual void, nor is it accomplished simply by the good intentions of the viewer. Rescue and Restore's call details the object on which the gaze rests, to seek out those "hidden among us." Sherene Razack has argued that relations of subordination and domination "stubbornly regulate" spaces of legal practice and knowledge production.[37] If migrants are in need of immigration relief, must they first be victimized and then cooperative in order to offer up a currency of exchange for legal status?[38] The position of victimhood maintained by law—notably, a position in which one is not made safe or saved by law—cannot do without criminalization, punishment, and crime, reinforced through what Kelli Moore has called legal spectatorship of the image and visuality of injury specific to legal schemes addressing gender-based violence.[39]

Rescue and Restore played a small but significant role in affirming public participation in *seeing like* police and calling the police—even when someone from the public knows nothing about the structures of immigration, sex work, migration, imperialism, global capitalism, or any of the conditions that shape people's lives.[40] As shown by Kaaryn Gustafson, there is a larger history of state welfare agencies functioning as outlets for the public to report and participate in surveillance of activity and behaviors that are purportedly suspicious or seemingly fraudulent, which does not necessarily result in structural changes and can create more chaotic outcomes for communities of color.[41] For example, the Anti-Trafficking in Persons Program spans across twenty-four different cities, regions, and states, involving nonprofit organizations, researchers, law enforcement, and other stakeholders.[42] While the projects, work areas, and services under the program encompass a wide range of focus areas, there is an emphasis on cooperative agreements that encourage public participation in the practice of identifying who may or may not be trafficked.

"See something say something" campaigns deputize the public into surveilling and reporting in ways that invite a racially charged version of civic duty for the public good. Without any knowledge of the political and economic conditions of gendered migration, the policing of sex work, or the consequences of

legal definitions of coercion, the public is invited to *act*. Ad campaigns in urban and rural cities, often on billboards, and in airports, alert the public to trafficking that was "hidden in plain sight." Images of shadowed women were often
circulated in ad campaigns. Julietta Hua has argued that such images produced
women's rights as universalisms anchored in dichotomies of victimhood and culpability that reproduce subjects of nation-state citizenship, rights, and political
economies.[43] Annie Fukushima has proposed a framing of migrants who cross
borders as witnessing trafficking, both the self-witness and that which is wit-
nessed, rather than being depleted or culpable.[44] Thus, the repetition of "Hidden in Plain Sight" as a campaign plea to the public establishes a never-ending
timeline: There can never be an eradication of what is already everywhere but
never seen. And the victim-subject is the cornerstone to this arrangement. For
example, the African American Policy Forum has argued that there is no existing state document which demonstrates a rise in human trafficking at sporting
events, yet heavy policing continues to impact Black communities at these events
and in surrounding neighborhoods and spaces.[45] Similarly, Lauren Martin and
Annie Hill have shown that between 2010 and 2016, over 76 percent of print
media sources linked the Super Bowl to human trafficking despite the absence
of any empirical data.[46]

QQ was a social work case manager in San Francisco for over two decades
and provided translation, social welfare, and health-related services for Asian
migrants who were undocumented and applying for T visa status. Trafficking
as an "issue area" did not organically emerge but rather became a part of her
work through racialized security partnerships initiated by federal antiterrorism programs designed to establish nonprofit collaborations. "This was after
9/11. Federal funds became available to us because antiterrorism, antitrafficking,
this is what they [federal agencies] cared about." Nadine Naber has argued that
post-9/11 policies rely not only on the racialization of Arab Americans, Mus-
lims, and South Asians in racial dichotomies of good/bad and citizen/terrorist
but also on political efforts to include immigrants in the security folds of the
nation-state. Leti Volpp has shown that antiterrorism policies anchored racial
figures of the "citizen" and the "terrorist" to expand the scope of immigration
law and the immigrant subject through the repositioning of Arab Americans as
always tied to terror and threats to US citizenship.[47] The punishment and policing of those racially marked through "terror" shift and challenge the humanitarian agendas of antitrafficking collaborations.

One of the more recent areas that involved QQ's participation was federal
immigration raids and the provision of services to Asian sex workers potentially

eligible for T status. Because of grant funding her organization received, QQ and staff at other nonprofit organizations were on call to provide services after a raid; this was how the organization came in contact with potential T status applicants. QQ described that advocates received forty-eight hours' notice and would then wait in the office for phone calls from the Federal Bureau of Investigation (FBI), then travel to a location and sometimes wait overnight. Everyone who was part of this effort worked with a nonprofit that received federal funding to provide social, legal, housing, and mental health services to those who had come in contact with immigration enforcement during a raid.

> When we're notified by the FBI that they are going to conduct a raid, we call volunteer interpreters and attorneys who are our partners. And then we wait.... After the raid, if there are twenty victims, we at least have to have five groups; each group has three people. So, it's fifteen people waiting there.... I keep on saying that this cannot solve the problem of course.... Imagine you are being investigated by some people with uniforms—FBI with big badges, walking around with guns. And then we come in and say we are the saviors: "We are here to help you, help you to try and get a green card, and we try to give you housing, and we get you benefits." The victims are so confused. Within twelve hours, there are two groups of people, one group saying, "I am going to kick you out of the country for doing 'illegal' things," and another group saying, "I am your savior; I am trying to save you" [sigh]. So, it's really interesting, all these procedures; it's interesting to look at all this and say, "Wow, something is going on."

QQ shared this story almost in a single breath. Her organization often partnered with the legal advocacy group with which I volunteered. Every story QQ shared about law was detailed with experiences of working with local police or federal immigration agencies to assist before a raid on a massage parlor or place of work, cooperate during a raid, and provide resources and services to women afterward: "There are two groups of people, one group saying, 'I am going to kick you out of the country...' and another group saying, 'I am your savior; I am trying to save you.'" QQ could not publicly participate in a political critique of immigration enforcement or police during this time because it might jeopardize client cases that relied on her own communication with law enforcement.

She went on to describe the moments after an immigration raid took place at a massage parlor, finding herself in a room with other advocates, as well as the FBI agents who had contacted their organization a few days before. "I keep on saying that this cannot solve the problem *of course*." As QQ explained, the problem is not merely the confusion produced by a targeted immigration raid but also the very scene of presumed cooperation in the room itself. The immigration raid is not a paradox of contradiction or conflation in which one promise is opposite another in law. Rather, it is a highly enforced and regulated space where social advocacy has meaning only in tension with its relationship to logics of punishment. We can imagine the many different ways to reduce harm in people's lives—for example, meeting basic needs for sustained and affordable housing, immediate crisis intervention, medical care, food assistance, mental health support, relationships of radical care, creativity, rest, support, and freedom from the criminalization of legal status. Antitrafficking laws are not designed for these needs, and if such needs are met, they are circumstantial.

It may be tempting to read cooperation between QQ's organization and immigration enforcement or local enforcement as a suspension of norms or a state of exception. And while she certainly did not equate her own organization with that of a state agency, QQ's articulation of a shaky stance—"we are here to help you"—is far from a state of exception in social service or advocacy work in our contemporary moment. Indeed, if we render the unfolding of cooperation as nothing more than a necessary practicality, we establish the same logic of law's willingness to create a temporary exception in order to further naturalize the use of punishment against communities of color.

Conclusion

ME: Some argue that advocacy work with survivors should not rely on the criminal legal system.

CL: I don't think I have a strong opinion.... I'm really torn about this because I've had clients ... if they had never been arrested and detained by immigration, and faced with the possibility that they would be deported, they would not have cooperated and in that way they would have never gotten the T visa. So for some of those clients, because they were forced to cooperate, they were given relief.... Do I think that's the kindest, gentlest way, to help people? No, no, of course not, and of course it should be someone's choice whether or not they want to cooperate. But that's not the system we have.... I don't know if I'd be in favor of totally taking away that stick provision. But on the flip side, this is trafficking advocacy; it is all about trying to help people regain their sense of agency, and it's kind of ironic that the starting point of that, after they leave the trafficking situation, would be a situation of coercion, do you know what I mean?

I return to CL's words here because what she did not know or felt unsure about was not the contradictions or negations of the precision, clarity, and intense detailed knowledge of the law and legal systems she possessed. To me, these moments reflected the kind of knowledge that is produced by the existing legal design that requires theorizing race, gender, and feminist politics. While no attorney or case manager interviewed in this chapter was actively involved in critiquing policing, they all articulated difficulty with securitization, criminalization, and border regulation in their efforts and struggles to focus on obtaining legal protection for those lacking legal status and surviving the harms of gender and sexual violence. It is my hope that the abolition feminist insights I present throughout this chapter help provide different language and possible practices to address the tensions set in place by neoliberal state structures.

Conclusion

ABOLITION FEMINISMS: REWRITING
THE VICTIM IN ANTI-ASIAN HATE

I've been a case manager for over ten years. I can help women with housing, getting
status, restraining orders.... These are all important, and that's why I am here.
But at the end of the day, this thing is still there—this thing about gender.

What if we had started with abolition?

These reflections come from two separate interviews conducted in the same
year. They are reflections of simultaneous beginnings and endings that are neither conclusive nor lacking. And each raises the kind of question that leads us
down the difficult path of accountability that can only come from collective
work. I share them here because they help me pause and concretely state one of
the concerns of this book: How have we lived with violence? The most central
worry of this book rests at the site of the victim in law—who can be legible in
law, how we talk about ourselves and see ourselves in this way, and what this

means for how we build or refuse institutions and relations with others. As Angela Davis, Gina Dent, Erica Meiners, and Beth Richie have written, abolition feminisms embody the "ability to look both inwards and outward" to obtain immediate demands and needs while also embracing the layered and complicated broadscale advocacy work beyond that immediacy. Further, these challenges are taken not as limitations but as "necessary sites for collective analysis"—never the singular solution.[1]

In 2022, following President Donald Trump's proclamation of the "Chinese virus" and "Kung flu," some political narratives spurred racist images and ideologies of foreignness and blamed Asianness for the global pandemic—and even more. The racial identity of Chinese people imposed onto bodies marked as Asian resulted in beatings, death, verbal assaults, and confrontations against elders, youth, children, and young women. In addition, national news sources documented an influx of white supremacist ideologies tied to xenophobia, Islamophobia, transphobia, and growing anti-Black and anti-immigrant politics. In response, some Asian American voices emerged to raise public awareness about these incidences under the political banner of "anti-Asian hate," defined as individual prejudice against Asians.

The politics of anti-Asian hate was the dominant mainstream framework at this time, and its political message was based in normative terms of criminality, a fervor to call on the police to advance policing of public spaces, and an uncritical invitation for more police to come into Asian American spaces. Anti-Asian Hate politics called upon the state to view Asian Americans specifically as victims of hate-crimes. During this time, it was certainly understandable that many were drawn to these political claims as they attempted to think about safety. But who really benefits and what power is built not just for individuals, but for communities, when the state will only pay attention to you if someone else properly hates you? This quick advance of a political agenda grew in a specific way—a reliance on an uncritical and unstated usage of victimhood and fear without careful political engagement with how we understand violence. Thus, if policing and collaborations with immigration enforcement continue to terrorize communities, what conditions would be expected of Asians in order to become legible as hate-based victims? If we think about the lessons abolition feminists and survivor centered frameworks have taught us, we might ask, what kind of exchange does the law accept in order for someone to become an exception to the larger structured violence of policing in the name of individual hate prejudice?

I recognize that certain politics such as #StopAPIHate focused on critiquing organized white supremacist groups and wide-scale orientalist and anti-immigrant messages used to scapegoat the Asian body for the global pandemic.

However, this political battle was also being fought by so many different Asian American and multiracial organizations (which were building mutual aid programs), de-escalation trainings, ethnic studies faculty and students, church groups, artists, writers, and a range of small- and large-scale efforts all attempting to do something in ways that would address harm—carefully and accountably. It is important to highlight that there were many other voices in Asian American political and community organizing circles that were not focused on individuals who hate, but instead, focused on systemic structures of anti-Asian violence. They called for community-driven care networks and harm-reduction strategies instead of narrowly focusing public resources on police collaborations to raise awareness about hate or databasing individual prejudice. The political claims of anti-Asian hate frameworks often resulted in data being passed to and from the state. How might these claims have looked if the focus on crime statistics had instead emerged differently, as a substantive engagement with the long-standing political movements that mobilized against criminalization, policing, and prisons? Or how might solutions designed to address attacks on our communities draw upon the strategies shared by Asian American feminists that critique the enforcement of victimhood, disability justice frameworks on safety and care? Or what Dean Spade, Craig Willse, and Chandan Reddy have shown in their critique of white normative gay rights activists who embraced racial and economic assimilationist narratives promoted by federal hate crimes legislation, such as the Shepard Byrd Act.[2] Grace Hong has argued that women of color feminist theorizations and activist thought are a politics of difference both within and across coalitional groups that drives much of the emergence of political strategy and formations of the moment as a genealogical legacy. In many ways the politics of anti-Asian hate erases the force of this work and results in what Hong has critiqued as a neoliberal disavowal.[3] In turning toward women of color feminisms, contemporary incidents of anti-Asian violence would be understood quite differently: not as mere prejudice or individualized hate, but rather as a death or racial violence that is a resistance and that requires a deeper theorization that does not valorize life against death because it simply cannot do so.

The discourse of anti-Asian hate was the first nationally televised framework showcasing Asian American communities to a wider audience during the COVID-19 pandemic—a white audience. During a political moment when global movements called for the defunding of police, lifting Asian and Asian American political voices through a pro-policing vein is nothing short of heartbreaking. When there has been hesitancy about policing, much of the criticism focuses only on the lack of response from police and the need for increased funding to continue the political project of policing, not to interrogate its terms.

Unfortunately, the discourse of anti-Asian hate has built itself on a committed interest in advancing criminalization of the hating subject and reification of continual demographic data of Asians as crime victims. To be clear, I am in no way disregarding the lives of those who have experienced and continued to experience violence. But I am arguing for a different orientation, and I am attempting to lift up the voices and writings of abolition feminisms that have taken pains to theorize violence. Oddly, violence is very much a main component of what should be theorized and politicized by the politics of anti-Asian hate, yet it is undertheorized and submerged under the prejudice and individualized hate frame.

How might an abolition feminist approach toward the legal subject of the hate-crime victim help us rethink and imagine a politics of not just individual safety but community safety? How might it even allow us to better demand resources and institutional or structural changes? For me, abolition feminisms push us to imagine beyond the making of punishment as necessary and, in doing so, require new ways of relating to ourselves, others, and the kinds of worlds we build while living through violence. As I hope this book has made clear, there is always violence in legibility. But this does not mean we cannot imagine, create, or relate in new ways. As elected officials and policy makers embrace *and also* reject acknowledgment of violence in the lives of Asian Americans, I hope that we can take seriously the lessons that have been made possible largely by the work of feminist and queer of color mobilizations against white mainstream feminist antiviolence movements.

State governments that have responded to the politics of "anti-Asian hate" have mostly responded with promises to provide more resources for police to protect victims, community partnerships with police to expand state programs to document hate crimes, and calls for cultural competency responses to "know" Asians better. But a continuing difficulty remains in the inability of "anti-Asian hate" discourse to develop an intellectual trajectory around race and/or violence that does not reproduce the rhetoric of state *solutions* or position Asian communities within the structure of proper victimhood. If, for example, state resources tied to social welfare, health, housing and shelter, and varying needs are only available if Asian Americans are first legible as victims of hate, then what does this say? "Hate crime" is a legal categorization, not an identity that communities create for themselves; it is imposed by the state onto people after they have experienced harm, and it is used to measure and determine the worth of that harm as a category of crime. In effect, the state demands that the resources, need, and violence Asian Americans experience are worthy of recognition through the legal production of victim. But the emphasis on individualized hate or prejudice minimalizes the harm Asian American communities experience because it assumes that the proper solution is to correct another individual, rather than to address structures of state violence. I want to be clear that I am in no way disregarding the longer political history of Asian American politics that struggled to gain recognition of Asian Americans as hate crime victims among the broader multiracial efforts to do the same. But I am saying that, because of this early set of struggles, many political and intellectual voices have since responded and critiqued the conditions put in place because of hate crimes logics.

When I think of this political moment, I think about the depth of what it means for Asian American politics to address different ways of knowing, being, and healing while also developing advocacy and client services that require resources. But further, on top of these components, there is an additional layer of having to combat the reformist politics of "anti-Asian hate" from within. I know many, including myself, who participated in small- and large-scale conversations to try and think through what could be done without furthering the neoliberal pulse of mainstream American interest in anti-Asian hate as somehow a "public safety" agenda. How was it that a non-Asian American "public" feigned interest in Asian American lives to then buttress the call for more policing particularly during a growing era of global uprising and "defund the police" political movements?

I am reminded of how difficult it was for feminists of color to enter conversations during this time. In "Beyond #StopAsianHate: Criminalization, Gender, and Asian Abolition Feminism," Hyejin Shim presents responses to anti-Asian hate that emerged from community activists working with survivors and family members of the Atlanta spa shootings in 2021, when a young white male murdered eight people, including six Asian women working at massage parlors where he had been a past customer. In this piece, they urge us to reflect on the politics of #StopAsianHate, which drew attention to the lives of those lost in Atlanta but did so by valorizing the victim and sanitizing sex work from the narrative as a form of respectability politics.[4] We might consider how anti-sex work and respectability politics that emerge here rely upon the "worthy victim" subject that is enforced by the larger discourse of protections bound to punishment discussed throughout this book. Because the specific "hate crime victim" is a legal subject, I hope that a critique of the racial and gendered conditions of this subject might also be an organizing possibility to address the racial logics of criminalization against race, sexuality, ability, and foreignness. That is, what exactly is the protection or benefit that is attached to the legal subject of the hate crime victim, what is the cost or expectation, and what other conditions are propelled in its wake?

Abolition feminist thinkers and organizers within and against mainstream antiviolence movements make possible a critique of "public safety" agendas that police race and sexuality against those marked as threats to heteronormative spaces of domestic whiteness. Asian American political claims that embrace public safety agendas are shocking, particularly given modern American legal productions that mark Asian bodies as foreign threats to be surveilled, which rely on the public safety policing tools that anti-Asian hate discourses inadvertently align with. As Ren-yo Hwang has argued, hate crimes law and policies have a long history of producing discourses of punishment against queer youth and Black communities that expanded California's carceral institutions.[5] Further, Hwang has turned our attention toward the particular shape of carceral feminist reforms that unfortunately establish a politics anchored in "rebranding, recruitment, and retraining" that repackage state institutions of racial violence such as policing and prisons into liberal "veneer-like" solutions toward rescue.[6] Similarly, Pooja Gehi and Soniya Munshi have shown that the Violence Against Women Act and hate crimes legislation embrace the same racial logic of Asian Americans as only victims in what they call "model-minority victims." Their work has shown that this racial logic of Asian American victimhood reproduces the model minority myth and its ongoing disavowal of communities targeted by antiterrorism laws and programs, surveillance, and US imperialism and wars in Asia and across the Pacific.[7] Dylan Rodríguez has critiqued anti-Asian hate campaigns for promoting "Asian American exceptionalism" as a vantage point that is detached from the larger history of US imperialism and colonialism. For Rodríguez, anti-Asian hate's political performativity inadvertently reproduces white nationalist narratives of individualism, racial capitalism, and prisons— the very same functions that fuel ongoing "domestic warfare" against communities of color.[8]

What I hope I put forward in this book is an embrace of the work and lives of abolitionist feminist thinkers as a genealogy that has already worked toward abolishing the legal subject of the crime victim through which the state enforces its claims on us. If we critique the ongoing presence of violence within the liberal state, then our politics will always center communities and people who stand to experience vulnerability at the hands of "reformist reforms," as Ruth Wilson Gilmore argues.[9] Gilmore reminds us that nonprofit organizations may promote themselves to be outside the state but may nonetheless enact policy reform efforts that mimic and reproduce the governing structures and ideology of the state itself. The problem with such reproduction lies in the uneven distribution of material resources that discursively divides communities and the cost that members outside of reputable nonprofit structures end up enduring, often without acknowledgment of that cost. "Reformist reform" politics can even emerge internally within nonprofit spaces that appear to be radical departures from reformist politics but are instead mere extensions.

Law enforcement public safety campaigns promise to reform the problem of crime, and immigration enforcement promises to resolve the problem of borders, and both are examples of *reform politics* that abolition feminists have argued should instead be seen as forms of state violence. To engage these state violences, this book focused on legal protection via policing, as an example of *reformist reform* laws and policies. Reformist reforms attempt to fix the initial reform that is often an outgrowth of the state. However, when these law and policy solutions also rely upon an insatiable requirement to racially correct Blackness, for example, they reproduce the violence of criminalization and policing by disavowing it and creating new legal subject positions, such as the assimilation of the undocumented crime victim. Mainstream violence against women and antitrafficking politics that reject any acknowledgment of the anti-Blackness of criminalization are examples of the main reformist reforms discussed in this book. In "What Justice Wants," Eve Tuck and K. Wayne Yang have argued that racial justice, or the political claims of justice invoked to address race and racism, tends toward a gaze on the state that is always wanting from the state.[10] That is, if justice is delivered by the state, then its terms will always start with the state and foreclose in this way. In thinking through the ongoing colonial formation of the nation-state, then, they ask what it would mean to reposition a politics of decolonization that moves against the limitations of justice as a "colonial temporality." Because one must always be legibly injured to then ask for justice from the state, there is a temporal logic or a "time" of the injured subject that shores up the static position of the administrative state, which is maintained and reinforced by *in*justice in its material form. Tuck and Yang draw on Stephen Best and Saidiya Hartman's writings that anti-Blackness is a regularity, a domination, and a terror exemplified in redress and reform, and often the very political strategies that promise to uphold or address justice will only address political issues that are already legible and recognizable to the state.[11]

Because the visibility of the victim continues to repeat, with regularity, in law and policy solutions, this book has not suggested that there is nothing beyond its dominant presence. Legal relief and benefits will continue to be delivered and used because legal protections *are enforced*; for this reason, I am not interested in blaming those who receive an enforced protection nor those who advocate for them. But what I am saying is that we can and must also continue to interrogate the terms of legal protection, refuse the promise of the singular solution, and reveal the lie that punishment delivers safety without the harm of racial violence. Turning toward abolition feminisms as a starting point is one way to shift political claims away from the solutions that reform the state through policing and prisons.

This book hopes to show that the legal subject of the victim is not made for survivors of gender and sexual violence; if so, then it is not made for Asian Americans communities as well because those who survive harm, and those who struggle to think through safety, are a part of our communities and multiple others as well. In other words, the abolition feminist critiques of mainstream antiviolence politics and the laws and policies that establish legal protection as bound to legal punishment can inform the direction of Asian American political claims—in particular, with regard to the place of policing and prisons. In this way, we think not about the singular solution that provides the next step, but about which solutions are already in place that must be unthought. The crime victim subject crosses into so many other areas of the liberal state that it continues to be relentlessly present in different forms of contemporary Asian American politics. For me, a critique of legal protection and its relationship to policing is necessary to address racial violence and to detach harm from the care and safety that collectives, communities, and people have been providing for each other.

Acknowledgments

Thank you to the anonymized nonprofit organizations and individuals who spoke with me during my research for this book. Important stages of my ideas developed through the Mellon Sawyer Workshop at the University of Washington; the University of Washington Bothell Interdisciplinary Arts and Sciences faculty lectures; the lecture series at the Center for Race and Gender at the University of California, Berkeley; and the Interdisciplinary Faculty Seminar on Race, Gender, Culture, and Community at the University of Hawai'i Manoa.

Alisa Bierria and Andrea Ritchie organized multiple abolition feminist dialogues with organizers, artists, and writers—I am thankful to have been part of these conversations, which shaped much of my thinking. Many of the questions I address are possible because of different parts of INCITE!'s collective political work against the nonprofit industrial complex, heteropatriarchy, prisons and policing, gender and sexual violence, imperialism, colonialism, and much more. I am particularly grateful to Alisa Bierria, Shana griffin and Zora, Mimi Kim, Beth Richie, Andrea Ritchie, Nadine Naber, Andrea Smith, Xandra Ibarra, Soniya Munshi, Kiri Sailiata, and Ujju Agarwal. Alisa Bierria and Shana griffin helped uplift ideas in this book even when I doubted myself.

At Duke University Press, Liz Ault provided encouragement and guidance throughout this entire process; thank you to Ben Kossak and Bird Williams, and the generous feedback from the two anonymous reviewers.

The Asian American Studies Center and the Center for the Study for Women at the University of California, Los Angeles (UCLA), provided faculty funding support. In the Department of Asian American Studies at UCLA, thank you to graduate student researchers Alyssa Hamamoto, Kristi Mai, and April Yang. Asian American studies department senior faculty support allowed for the completion of this book; thank you to Victor Bascara, Lucy Burns, Keith

Camacho, Jennifer Chung, Grace Hong, Purnima Mankekar, Natalie Masuoka, Valerie Matsumoto, Karen Umemoto, David Yoo, and Min Zhou; and thank you to colleagues Jolie Chea, Evyn Lê Espiritu Gandhi, Nour Joudah, Valerie Matsumoto, Thu-hương Nguyễn-võ, Kyeyoung Park, Loubna Qutami, Renee Tajima-Peña, and Cindy Sangalang, and department administrators Wendy Fujinami, Justin Dela Cruz, and Xuan-Mai Vo. At UCLA, thank you to Alisa Bierria for reminding me about the why, Colby Lenz for the work and hidden humor, Grace Hong and Jennifer Chung for institutional guidance, yoga/best food writing combos with Wendy Sung, and work sessions with Ayasha Guerin; thank you to Jolie Chea especially during the first year, gummy bears, and cards; and Lucy Burns for check-ins and the reminder of well-being. I am grateful for Juliann Anesi, Amy Ritterbusch, Carlos Santos, and Latoya Small during early transitions to campus.

At different stages, I am thankful for comments and feedback from Chandan Reddy, Dean Spade, Alex Weheliye, Denise Ferreira da Silva, Wayne Yang, Jin Haritaworn, and Tiffany Willoughby-Herard. Thank you to Laura Kang, Susette Min, and Leti Volpp for collaborative project opportunities on anti-Asian violence. Thank you to Leti Volpp for postdoctoral guidance at the University of California, Berkeley. Gillian Harkins and Rana Jaleel provided important opportunities to discuss law and violence in interdisciplinary contexts. During the early stages of my thinking, presentations with Chris Finely, Angie Morrill, Soniya Munshi, Maile Arvin, Kit Myers, Ren-yo Hwang, and Kiri Sailiata helped shape my trajectory. Maryam Griffin and Thea Quiray Tagle were both anchors during major transitions in life and institutions.

Research and writing began while I was a graduate student at the University of Michigan; thank you to Nadine Naber, Sarita See, Andrea Smith, and Sora Han for guidance both within and beyond the academy. Thank you to Marlene. Chris Finley continues to encourage me and work through ideas, and is a Costco buddy; thank you to Kiri Sailiata for supporting family, writing retreats, and reading drafts. I'm thankful for time with Lani Teves, Kelley Fayard, Mindy Mizobe, Lloyd Grieger, Jesse Car, Isabel Millan, Navaneetha Mokkil, Jessi Gan, Melia Sailiata, Manan Desai and Retika Adhikari, Matt and Jourdan Stiffler, Eric Shih and Hai-Binh Nguyen, and the Detroit Asian Youth Project: Michelle Lin, Scott Kurashige, Emily Lawsin, Marcia Lee, Stephanie Chang, Hugo Shih, Soh Suzuki, and my time as a community volunteer with Asian Prisoner Support Committee and Creative Interventions.

I'm always grateful for Megan Francis, the OG, loudest and greatest, always grounding and reminding me of where I come from and its importance to this work; thank you to Frank William Miller Jr. for cat respect and creativity. Mindy

Mizobe helped me through many different moments in life; thank you, Mindy and Lloyd Greiger for always knowing the Wang texts. While in Honolulu, I am thankful for Mike Nakasone, Lani Teves, Lianne Rozelle, Dawn and Genevive, Joyce Mariano, and Kate Kane. Karin Mak and Neel Garlapati provided feedback and midweek lunch breaks during the last stages of writing. Janice Chou sent support messages, and Weston Teruya helped discuss different ideas. Wendy and Randy provided support with family and home during writing stages, and thank you to Christina and Logan for check-ins. Thank you to Chris Reed and Crystal Shield for support at critical moments and Kim Greenwell and Craig Willse for editing and feedback. Vanara Taing and I have continually supported each other's creativity and writing over decades, and thank you to Asaph for the many stories.

I thank my parents, especially my mom, who reminds me about why the kind parts of me are there, and my brother for checking in on me. Luna II was with me through every single moment. I thank my loving partner Brian Chung for supporting me through each stage in the process, pushing healthy meals, listening to repeats, bringing all the jokes, and making me take breaks.

I thank myself, and it took me a while to realize that.

Notes

INTRODUCTION

1. See Silliman and Bhattacharjee, *Policing the National Body*; and Lindsley, "Gendered Assault on Immigration." For a discussion of the historical legacy of systems of immigration control, incarceration, and colonialism, see Hernández, *City of Inmates*.

2. I use the word *immigrant* when I am referring to a set of political movements (as in the phrase *immigrant rights*) or a set of community politics that have already identified as such and when referring to a subject position within the law. When this book analyzes nonimmigrant visas in comparison to immigrant visas, these two categories of visas are determined by the state's management of legal status. I write with the word *undocumented* because I am analyzing the politics around the absence of legal status as opposed to the legal definition of unauthorized aliens, and the political frameworks that have developed in relation to these existing legal categories. When referring to undocumented survivors, I am aligning with political movements to lift up those without legal status and to critique the very terms of enforcement that regulate status. I also use the word *migrant* to refer to people who have experienced the forced displacement and movement of peoples across nation-state borders. This book is in no way interested in measuring behaviors or characteristics related to any group of people categorized by such terms.

3. Budd, "Incarcerated Women and Girls."

4. Swavola et al., *Overlooked*; American Civil Liberties Union, "Prison Rape Elimination Act"; and Dholakia, "Women's Incarceration Rates."

5. The work of organizers and writers who have made this analysis possible is vast. See the community accountability statements from INCITE! Women of Color Against Violence and Critical Resistance and collectives of writings in INCITE!, *Color of Violence*; INCITE!, *Revolution Will Not Be Funded*; Chen et al., *Revolution Starts at Home* ; Kaba and Hassan, *Fumbling Towards Repair*; Dixon and Piepzna-Samarasinha, *Beyond Survival*; and Ben-Moshe, *Decarcerating Disability*. For me, INCITE! and the work of Survived and Punished and Creative Interventions anchors my focus on political movement building in relation to advocacy, service, and the everyday.

6. Sokoloff and Pearce, "Locking Up Hope."

7. Bhuyan, "'Battered Immigrant'"; and Kwong, "Removing Barriers."

8. Thuma, *All Our Trials*.

9. In addition, Elizabeth Bernstein has argued that carceral logics are embedded in feminist humanitarian projects reliant on Western moral and religious campaigns aligned with the expansion of nation-state borders. Bumiller, *In an Abusive State*; Goodmark, *Troubled Marriage*; Bernstein, *Brokered Subjects*; and Bernstein, "Militarized Humanitarianism."

10. The statement was released at the height of the global uprisings for Black lives in the wake of political organizing against the Minneapolis police murder of George Floyd and the many Black deaths by the carceral state.

11. Regarding neoliberal political and economic restructuring, and the limits of political strategies that aim to include queer and trans communities in existing administrative violences, see Spade, *Normal Life*. For additional discussion of alternative organizing strategies, namely, mutual aid as a political practice, see Spade, *Mutual Aid*. For discussion of multiculturalism in US political discourse and racial representation, neoliberalism, and the liberal state form, see Melamed, *Represent and Destroy*.

12. M. Kim et al., *Abolition and Social Work*; Roberts, *Shattered Bonds*; and Roberts, *Killing the Black Body*.

13. See Finley, "Ghostly Care," writing on Leanne Betasamosake Simpson's decolonial love. See also Piepzna-Samarasinha, *Care Work*. Leah Lakshmi Piepzna-Samarasinha has asked what it would mean to have a collective responsibility toward care, in writing about ableism in community organizing work, as well as engagements with the state, and uplifting the work of disability justice and disabled queer folks of color.

14. As I discuss throughout this book, even though VAWA provisions currently do not restrict applicants or recipients based on their gender, race, or sexuality, it is the sign of woman (or more specifically the damage unto woman) that is often the subject of political debates on public safety, punishment, and legislative debates surrounding VAWA. I will refer to *women* or *woman* throughout my discussion because the advocates I interviewed primarily served Asian immigrant women and their communities. Victims of Violence Against Women Act, Pub. L. No. 103-322, tit. IV, § 40001, 108 Stat. 1902 (1994), and the Violence Protection Act of 2000, Pub. L. No. 106-386, 114 Stat. 1464 (2000).

15. Capps et al., *Profile of U.S. Children*. The 1994 VAWA allowed benefits and eligibility for benefits and the possibility to self-petition for legal permanent resident status, which is a form of legal status, without having to rely on the citizen or legal permanent resident who originally sponsored them (and could be causing them harm).

16. Gilmore, *Abolition Geography*, 484.

17. Matsuda, *Where Is Your Body?*, 40–41. Matsuda writes specifically on the targeted criminalization of Black men.

18. Farley writes, "White-over-black is a desire, an orientation. It is the result of a training." Farley, "Accumulation," 58.

19. Haley, "Flesh Work."

20. Garcia, "'All Canned Foods.'"

21. Melamed and Reddy, "Using Liberal Rights."

22. Harris writes that property does not precede law, that property is itself a legal con-

struct that protects expectations, measures those, and values those expectations as property. "In fact, the difficulty lies not in identifying expectations as part of property, but in distinguishing which expectations are reasonable and therefore merit the protection of the law as property. Although the existence of certain property rights may seem self-evident and the protection of certain expectations may seem essential for social stability, property is a legal construct by which selected private interests are protected and upheld." Harris, "Whiteness as Property," 1729–30.

23. Mahoney, "Failure to Protect Laws."

24. Prah, "Domestic Violence."

25. Oparah, *Global Lockdown*.

26. Komar et al., *Sentencing Reform*. See also Stoever, *Politicization of Safety*; and Goodmark, *Imperfect Victims*.

27. Bierria and Lenz, *Defending Self-Defense*.

28. Bierria and Lenz, "Battering Court Syndrome."

29. M. Kim, "From Carceral Feminism"; and M. Kim et al., "World Without Walls."

30. M. Kim, "From Carceral Feminism."

31. Richie, "Reimagining the Movement."

32. Richie, *Arrested Justice*.

33. Bierria, "Missing in Action."

34. Women of color feminists working early on within antiviolence movements have argued that gender and sexual violence is symptomatic of racial capitalism, colonialism, war, and imperialism, rather than intrinsic to individual behavior. See INCITE!, *Color of Violence*; INCITE! and Critical Resistance, "Statement on Gender Violence"; INCITE!, *Revolution Will Not Be Funded*; and Oparah, "Rethinking Antiviolence Strategies."

35. Munshi, "Multiplicities of Violence."

36. Richie et al., "Colluding."

37. Mijente et al., *Who's Behind ICE?*

38. Ritchie, *Invisible No More*.

39. Simon, *Governing Through Crime*; and Gottschalk, *Prison and the Gallows*.

40. Bierria, "Missing in Action." See also Celeste Winston's discussion of abolition and public safety agendas, Black flight and placemaking, and theorization of marronage. Winston, *Lose the Hounds*.

41. Violent Crime Control and Law Enforcement Act, Pub. L. No. 103-322, 108 Stat. 1796 (1994); and Violence Against Women Act, Pub. L. No. 103-322, tit. IV, § 40001, 108 Stat. 1902 (1994). The majority of grants funded through VAWA are administered by the Office on Violence Against Women. The reauthorization in 2022 extended existing programs and created additional programs to expand what qualified as criminal activity, established tribal authority to enforce tribal laws pertaining to gender-based violence and related crimes under certain conditions, expanded tribal criminal jurisdiction over those marked as non-Indian, increased territories' eligibility for grant programs, established new provisions for rape kit backlogs, and enhanced measures focused on trafficking in persons and sex trafficking, to name just a few.

42. For a breakdown of all VAWA appropriations in the 2013 reauthorization and a

summary of prior reauthorizations, see Hanson and Sacco, "Violence Against Women Act (VAWA) Reauthorization"; and Kemper and Sacco, *The Violence Against Women Act (VAWA)*.

43. VAWA authorized $215 million in 2019, $215 million in 2020, $215 million in 2021, $217 million in 2022, and $255 million in 2023 to STOP (Services, Training Officers, and Prosecutors) Violence Against Women Formula Grants. See Kemper, *The 2022 Violence Against Women Act (VAWA) Reauthorization*.

44. A full summary is available in Kemper, *The 2022 Violence Against Women Act (VAWA) Reauthorization*.

45. Violent Crime Control and Law Enforcement Act of 1994, Title I: Public Safety and Policing.

46. Personal Responsibility and Work Opportunity Reconciliation Act of 1996, Pub. L. No. 104-193, 110 Stat. 2105 (1996).

47. Gustafson, *Cheating Welfare*; and Gustafson, "Degradation Ceremonies."

48. Roberts, *Killing the Black Body*; and Roberts, *Shattered Bonds*.

49. Ocen, "New Racially Restrictive Covenant"; and Ocen, "Punishing Pregnancy."

50. Kandaswamy, *Domestic Contradictions*; Hinton, *From the War on Poverty*; Fujiwara, *Mothers Without Citizenship*; and Park, "Challenging Public Charge Policy."

51. Perreira and Pedroza, "Policies of Exclusion"; Fortuny and Chaudry, *Overview of Immigrants' Eligibility*; and Abrego et al., "Making Immigrants into Criminals."

52. Macías-Rojas, "Immigration"; and Macías-Rojas, *From Deportation to Prison*.

53. Mostly legislated through the Battered Immigrant Women Protection Act of 2000, which reauthorized VAWA, these provisions are, generally, the ability for survivors to self-petition to become lawful permanent residents (green card) without relying on a US citizen or another legal permanent resident for the application, a waiver of inadmissibility, temporary legal status, derivative status for family members, and in some cases assistance with housing and work authorization. VAWA self-petition applicants must be victims of battery or extreme cruelty committed by a US citizen spouse or former spouse, parent, child, or lawful permanent resident spouse, former spouse, or parent in order to be eligible to self-petition for permanent resident status. In some cases, the applicant does not have to be married. Grounds for inadmissibility can impact whether someone is eligible. There is no annual cap on the number of VAWA self-petitions that can be approved. See U.S. Citizenship and Immigration Services, "Green Card for VAWA Self-Petitioner"; and the Battered Immigrant Women Protection Act, Pub. L. No. 106-386, tit. V, 114 Stat. 1464 (2000).

54. Walia, *Undoing Border Imperialism*.

55. Paik, *Bans, Walls, Raids, Sanctuary*.

56. For discussion of queer migrant social movements and collectives organizing and responding to heteronormative structures of border regulation and management, see Luibhéid and Chávez, *Queer and Trans Migrations*; and Chávez, *Queer Migration Politics*. On the role sexuality plays in immigration agencies, borders, and control, see Luibhéid, *Entry Denied*.

57. Motomura, *Immigration Outside the Law*.

58. Immigrant Responsibility Act of 1996, Pub. L. No. 104-208, 110 Stat. 3009 (1996);

Antiterrorism and Effective Death Penalty Act of 1996, Pub. L. No. 104-132, 110 Stat. 1214 (1996).

59. See Abrego et al., "Making Immigrants into Criminals."

60. Kerwin, "From IIRIRA to Trump."

61. Cházaro, "Challenging the 'Criminal Alien.'"

62. Chacón, "Producing Liminal Legality."

63. Escobar, *Captivity Beyond Prisons*. See also Chacón, "Managing Migration Through Crime."

64. Abrego et al., "Making Immigrants into Criminals"; Escobar, *Captivity Beyond Prisons*; Abrego, *Sacrificing Families*; and Abrego and Negrón-Gonzales, *We Are Not Dreamers*.

65. Jaleel, *Work of Rape*.

66. See Volpp, "The Citizen and the Terrorist"; Abu-Lughod et al., *Cunning of Gender Violence*; Dubrofsky and Magnet, *Feminist Surveillance Studies*; Maira, "'Good' and 'Bad' Muslim"; Abdulhadi et al., *Arab and Arab American Feminisms*; Jamal and Naber, *Race and Arab Americans*; and Naber, *Arab America*.

67. Naber, "Decolonizing Culture"; Naber, *Arab America*; and Naber, "So Our History."

68. Volpp, "(Mis)Identifying Culture"; Volpp, "Blaming Culture"; and Volpp, "Framing Cultural Difference."

69. Razack, "'Simple Logic'"; Razack, "Domestic Violence"; and Fellows and Razack, "Race to Innocence."

70. Davis et al., *Abolition. Feminism. Now*, 34.

71. Bierria et al., "Introduction," 1.

72. Existing scholarship has critiqued "cultural competency," and I certainly am in line with these arguments. However, here I focus on the violences that arise in the matching up of experience to the legal subject.

73. By *legal fiction*, I do not mean literary studies of law in works of fiction or socio-logical and legal studies writings that aim to identify fictitious or factually insubstantial claims or racial misrepresentations.

74. Kang, *Compositional Subjects*, 163.

75. Scott, "Evidence of Experience."

76. Darian-Smith, "Ethnographies of Law."

77. See Coutin, *Legalizing Moves*; and Coutin, *Exiled Home*.

78. Yngvesson and Coutin, "Schrödinger's Cat."

79. Ferreira da Silva, "Towards a Critique."

80. Han, *Letters of the Law*, 2.

81. All individuals and organizations mentioned here remain anonymous. I conducted semistructured interviews and participant observation from 2010 to 2012 and follow-up interviews in 2013.

82. Portions of this chapter were originally published in my 2016 article "Unsettling Innocence: Rewriting the Law's Invention of Immigrant Woman as Cooperator and Criminal Enforcer."

83. Dylan Rodríguez has argued for the need for critical excavation of certain theories

of exceptionalism and paradigms entrenched within the field. Rodríguez, "Asian American Studies."

1. WRITING AGAINST LEGAL FICTIONS

1. Arvin et al., "Decolonizing Feminism."

2. Scott, "Evidence of Experience."

3. For discussion on the nonprofit industrial complex and the measurements that police success, see Koyama, "Disloyal to Feminism"; and Oparah, "Rethinking Antiviolence Strategies." For discussion of damage-based frameworks, see Tuck, "Suspending Damage." Transnational feminist writers, third world feminists, and postcolonial critiques have brought forward writings to think through this difficulty. See also Amireh, "Palestinian Women's Disappearing Act"; Hemmings, *Why Stories Matter*; and Spivak, *Can the Subaltern Speak?*

4. Georgis, *Better Story*.

5. Hartman, "Venus in Two Acts," 11.

6. L. Smith, *Decolonizing Methodologies*, 37, 35.

7. Grace Carson has argued that policing and incarceration have always played a role in US colonial legal formations and thus limit tribal sovereignty. Sarah Deer argues that sexual violence is relevant to tribal sovereignty because tactics of sexual violence were used as part of colonial violences against Indigenous peoples and, most explicitly, that VAWA has been a site where federal agencies established jurisdictional authority over tribal courts and the lives of Indigenous survivors. Carson, "Tribal Sovereignty"; Deer, *Beginning and End of Rape*. See also Deer, "Decolonizing Rape Law." For further discussions on white feminist "violence against women" approaches and Indigenous feminist critique, see Hunt, "Representing Colonial Violence"; and Moreton-Robinson, *Talkin' Up*.

8. Simpson, "On Ethnographic Refusal."

9. Million, *Therapeutic Nations*, 86.

10. Hartman, *Scenes of Subjection*, 79.

11. Hong, "Intersectionality and Incommensurability." See also Hong, *Death Beyond Disavowal*.

12. Han analyzes *Gong Lum v. Rice* (275 U.S. 78 [1927]) and the legal claims of the Chinese plaintiffs, who, in Han's reading, argued against segregated schools because they were not allowed to enroll in an all-white school and be protected from Black people equally to the way white people were protected. While some have memorialized this case as an example of Asian Americans resisting the power of law, Han provides a different reading. As Han critiques, Asian American jurisprudence in this example defines itself against discrimination not through a white/not-white but a Black/not-Black claim. Han, "Politics of Race."

13. Han, *Letters of the Law*, 11.

14. Weheliye, *Habeas Viscus*, 4.

15. Samera Esmeir has also written on the juridical humanity of colonialisms. Esmeir, *Juridical Humanity*.

16. Crenshaw, "Mapping the Margins." See also Crenshaw, "Demarginalizing the Intersection."

17. Crenshaw, "Demarginalizing the Intersection."

18. Crenshaw, "Mapping the Margins."

19. Ocen, "Unshackling Intersectionality."

20. Ferreira da Silva, "Towards a Critique," 429. See also Ferreira da Silva, *Global Idea of Race*.

21. The form of law that Williams focuses on here is that of property. She writes, "My students, most of whom signed up expecting to experience that crisp, refreshing, clear-headed sensation that 'thinking like a lawyer' purportedly endows, are confused by this and all the stories I tell them in my class on Women and Notions of Property. They are... paralyzed by the idea that property might have a gender and that gender might be a matter of words." Williams, *Alchemy of Race and Rights*, 13.

22. Elia et al., *Critical Ethnic Studies*.

23. Han, *Letters of the Law*, 10.

24. Han, *Letters of the Law*, 10.

25. Han, *Letters of the Law*, 10.

26. Han, *Letters of the Law*, 10.

27. Han, *Letters of the Law*, 15.

28. Ferreira da Silva, "Towards a Critique," 423.

29. Ferreira da Silva, "Towards a Critique," 426.

30. I position legal practice within the broader history of laws set in place to limit the scope, reach, and impact of progressive lawyering and the kinds of work nonprofit legal centers are able to uphold in resisting the nonprofit industrial complex. See INCITE!, *Revolution Will Not Be Funded*.

Often, we address movements only when they are already evidence for the analyses we have set out to provide. Or, we conveniently use other movements that we find lacking in evidence to serve as reference points for those we do not wish to align with. This method of writing, whether recognizable as ethnographic or not, is rampant throughout literary, anthropological, cultural, and social scientific texts and unwittingly adopts a liberal placement of radical movements and peoples. Movements and organizations are referentially glossed without any critical engagement with the elements of organizing and the theories they make possible (whether in agreement or not). Further, this approach relies on a reading of movements and organizations as whole, discrete, unchanging, and insular objects. This is a violent form of erasure encouraged by neoliberal logics of scholarship and research that seek to delegitimize the intellectualism of movements and their legacies. Further, this move falsely renders creative and accountable ways of writing with and about movements as risky. We can resist this move by regarding the onto-epistemological struggles in organizing work as struggles that we can take up in our writing as a method of theory.

31. Cover, *Narrative, Violence*.

32. Constable, *Just Silences*, 59.

33. Constable, *Our Word*, 4.

34. Naimou, *Salvage Work*, 2.

35. Dayan, *Law Is a White Dog*, 32.

36. Naimou, *Salvage Work*, 4.

37. Young, *Illegible Will*, 3.

38. Abu-Lughod, "Can There Be?"

39. Narayan, "Ethnography and Fiction."

40. These analyses already exist of law and do not require a separate notion of legal fiction.

41. Visweswaran, *Fictions of Feminist Ethnography*. For related discussions, see Trinh, *Woman, Native, Other*; and Trinh, "Not You/Like You." See also Abu-Lughod, "Can There Be?"; and Abu-Lughod, "Do Muslim Women?"

2. MAKING THE UNDOCUMENTED CRIME VICTIM

1. Interview conducted in 2011. The category of "nonimmigrant status" is defined as a temporary immigration benefit, as opposed to "immigrant status." Throughout this chapter I use *U nonimmigrant status* and the more common term *U visa* interchangeably. U nonimmigrant status is not a visa typically issued by the State Department; it is a temporary legal benefit conferred by the Department of Homeland Security.

2. Victims of Trafficking and Violence Protection Act of 2000, Pub. L. No. 106-386, 114 Stat. 1464 (2000). The attorney general can consider converting nonimmigrant status to legal permanent resident status if doing so furthers "humanitarian interests."

3. Bumiller, *In an Abusive State*; Goodmark, *Troubled Marriage*; and Goodmark, *Imperfect Victims*.

4. M. Kim, "Carceral Creep."

5. Hanhardt, *Safe Space*.

6. Stoever, *Politicization of Safety*.

7. Richie, *Arrested Justice*; see also Ritchie, "Law Enforcement Violence"; Ritchie, *Invisible No More*; Ritchie and Jones-Brown, "Policing Race, Gender"; and Mogul et al., *Queer In(Justice)*.

8. Dasgupta and Eng, *Safety and Justice*; and Amnesty International, *Maze of Injustice*.

9. Rojas et al., "Community Accountability"; M. Kim et al., "World Without Walls"; Dixon and Piepzna-Samarasinha, *Beyond Survival*; Davis, "Race and Criminalization"; Davis and Shaylor, "Race, Gender"; Davis, *Are Prisons Obsolete?*; and Davis et al., *Abolition. Feminism. Now.*

10. INCITE!, *Color of Violence*; INCITE! and Critical Resistance, "Statement on Gender Violence"; INCITE!, *Revolution Will Not Be Funded*; Bierria et al., introduction; N. Smith and Stanley, *Captive Genders*; and Haritaworn et al., *Marvellous Grounds*.

11. Oparah, *Global Lockdown*; and Oparah, "Rethinking Antiviolence Strategies."

12. Ivie and Nanasi, "U Visa," 10.

13. Email communication on file with author. The magazine generates news articles reporting on trends in the field, and emerging issues that are pertinent to the staff and business operations of the agency. Each month, copies of the bulletin are distributed to police chiefs, sheriffs, National Academy graduates, libraries, and leading members of the agency. The first magazine issue was published in 1932 in the United States. In 2012, the bulletin was distributed to over 150 countries, was available online, and estimated a readership of approximately 200,000.

14. Ivie and Nanasi, "U Visa," 15.

15. Herman et al., *Bringing Victims*; and Harcourt, *Illusion of Order*. For federal agency documentation, see US Department of Justice, Office of Community Oriented Policing Services, *Enhancing Community Policing*; and Comrie and Elkins, *Reducing Crime*.

16. Two primary options were created, U and T status. In this chapter I focus on U status. "Alien Victims of Certain Qualifying Criminal Activity," 8 C.F.R. § 214.14. At the time of this book's writing, qualifying criminal activity includes attempts at the following: abduction, abusive sexual content, blackmail, domestic violence, extortion, false imprisonment, female genital mutilation, felonious assault, hostage, incest, involuntary servitude, kidnapping, manslaughter, murder, obstruction of justice, peonage, perjury, prostitution, rape, sexual assault, sexual exploitation, slave trade, torture, trafficking, witness tampering, unlawful criminal restraint, and other related crimes where the elements of the crime are substantially similar or attempts, conspiracy, or solicitation to commit any of the including categories. For a summary of VAWA immigrant provisions, see Kaguyutan et al., "Violence Against Women Act"; and Orloff and Kaguyutan, "Offering a Helping Hand." The Congressional Research Service has published several summaries of VAWA funding; see Kemper and Sacco, *Violence Against Women Act*.

17. Hallett, "Temporary Protection."

18. US Citizenship and Immigration Services, "Victims of Criminal Activity." See also US Citizenship and Immigration Services, *Trends*.

19. Current statutory language specifies that a "certifying official" from a qualifying agency must sign a form stating that applicants are "helpful, and currently being helpful, or will likely be helpful in the investigation of the case." See Kamhi and Lakhani, *Guide to State Laws*; and US Department of Homeland Security, "U and T Visa."

20. US Department of Homeland Security, Citizenship and Immigration Services, Office of Performance and Quality, "Number of Form I-918."

21. During the Subcommittee on Immigration and Claims hearing on the Battered Immigrant Women Protection Act, advocates and nonprofit directors spoke about the challenges noncitizen survivors faced if required to cooperate with prosecution specifically and in general when law enforcement are involved in protections. See US House of Representatives, Subcommittee on Immigration and Claims, *Battered Immigrant Women Protection Act of 1999: Hearing on HR 3083*, 106th Cong., 2nd Sess., July 20, 2000. For further discussion on the U Visa, see Orloff et al., "Mandatory U-Visa Certification."

22. US Citizenship and Immigration Services, *U Visa Demographics*. The report utilized demographic data from the USCIS electronic system and physical records on U visa principal petitioners and derivatives filing between fiscal years 2012 and 2018.

23. US Citizenship and Immigration Services, *U Visa Filing Trends*; and US Citizenship and Immigration Services, *Trends*.

24. For discussion of immigration law and criminal enforcement, see Chacón, "Managing Migration Through Crime"; and Chacón, "Producing Liminal Legality."

25. Haritaworn et al., "Murderous Inclusions." See also Bracke, "From 'Saving Women.'"

26. Stanley, *Atmospheres of Violence*.

27. Gilmore, "Abolition Geography and the Problem of Innocence," 234.

28. Gilmore, "Abolition Geography and the Problem of Innocence," 234.

29. Battered Immigrant Women Protection Act of 1999, Pub. L. No. 106-386, tit. V, §

1501, 114 Stat. 1518 (2000). See also Orloff et al., "Mandatory U-Visa Certification," arguing that VAWA's "any credible evidence" standard of proof should apply to other protections such as the U visa. The authors also argue that a certification requirement is a deterrent for filing an application for U status.

30. "Black Introduces."

31. Reddy, *Freedom with Violence*. See also Spade, *Normal Life*.

32. Ritchie, *Invisible No More*.

33. Rodríguez, "Asian American Studies."

34. Nadine Naber has shown that the domestic space of surveillance is a form of empire where security mechanisms construct racial hierarchies among "good" and "bad" immigrants that could otherwise be relations based on collective histories and solidarities. Naber, "'Look'"; and Naber, "So Our History."

35. Gehi and Munshi, "Connecting State Violence."

3. THE CONTRACTABLE VICTIM

1. See, for example, Hua, *Trafficking Women's Human Rights*; Kempadoo et al., *Trafficking and Prostitution Reconsidered*; US Department of State, *Human Smuggling and Trafficking Center*; and Bernstein, "Militarized Humanitarianism."

2. Kempadoo et al., *Trafficking and Prostitution Reconsidered*. See also Kempadoo and Doezema, *Global Sex Workers*.

3. Jaleel, *Work of Rape*.

4. Kang, *Traffic in Asian Women*.

5. Suchland, *Economies of Violence*.

6. Victims of Trafficking and Violence Protection Act of 2000, Pub. L. No. 106-386, 114 Stat. 1464 (2000). Like the U immigrant status, T nonimmigrant status is a temporary benefit most often granted to those already in the United States.

7. US Citizenship and Immigration Services, "Victims of Human Trafficking"; *Victims of Trafficking and Violence Protection Act of 2000*.

8. *Victims of Trafficking and Violence Protection Act of 2000*. The act allows for cooperation differences for persons under the age of eighteen or those physically or psychologically unable to due to trauma. It also contains guidelines around the waiver of inadmissibility.

9. US Citizenship and Immigration Services, "Victims of Human Trafficking."

10. US Department of Health and Human Services, *Services Available to Victims*.

11. In 2008 USCIS reported receiving 389 T visa applications, and in 2021, 1,702 applications. Even with the increase, the number comes nowhere near the 5,000 annual cap. US Department of Homeland Security, Citizenship and Immigration Services, Office of Performance and Quality, "Number of Form I-914, Application."

12. Charles Song and Suzy Lee argue that survivors should not have to cooperate because (1) they are usually already willing to prosecute the person doing harm, (2) prosecutors already have enforcement tools they need and survivor cooperation is superfluous, (3) requiring cooperation can result in unintended consequences beyond the original congressional intention to help women. However, we must also see that the willingness

of survivors is not concrete and whole, that coercion by law enforcement exemplifies the conditions of required cooperation, and that congressional intention around these visa schemes was not primarily intended to "help" women but to improve and expand enforcement power. Song and Lee, "Between a Sharp Rock."

13. All names of individuals and organizations are anonymous in this chapter and throughout this book.

14. Bernstein, "Militarized Humanitarianism." See also Bernstein, *Temporarily Yours.*

15. Shih, "Fantasy of Spotting." See also Shih, *Manufacturing Freedom.*

16. Brown, *States of Injury.*

17. Weheliye, *Habeas Viscus*, 77.

18. For a summary of the range of antitrafficking funds and grants tied specifically to victim services, see Finklea, "Trafficking in Persons."

19. Dahlstrom, "Trafficking and the Shallow State," 66. Dahlstrom cites "shallow state" bureaucratic barriers within the T visa process and calculates 42.79 percent denials of all T visa applications adjudicated in 2020 compared to 28.12 percent in 2015.

20. Dahlstrom, "Trafficking and the Shallow State," 68–69.

21. Between 2008 and 2021, the highest number of T visas granted was in 2021, with 1,430 applications approved out of 5,000 available. See US Citizenship and Immigration Services, *Characteristics of T Nonimmigrant Status.*

22. Chacón, "Tensions and Trade-Offs."

23. Deer, "Relocation Revisited"; and Hunt, "Representing Colonial Violence."

24. Chacón, "Managing Migration Through Crime"; and Chacón, "Tensions and Trade-Offs."

25. Hill, "Rhetoric of Modern-Day Slavery."

26. To be clear, I am not arguing that stories are where race lies because of the existence of people's lived experience but rather that the stories of those who attempt to use the law for others reveal the possibilities and limitations set forth by law's own design.

27. US Senate, Committee on Foreign Relations, *The Global Fight to End Modern Slavery: Hearing Before the Committee on Foreign Relations*, 115th Cong., 2nd Sess., November 28, 2018 (prepared statement of Shawna Bader Blau, Solidarity Center).

28. Funding is in the range of $75–$100 million.

29. Bernstein, "Sexual Politics."

30. Beutin, *Trafficking in Antiblackness.*

31. Maynard, "#Blacksexworkerslivesmatter." See also Maynard, *Policing Black Lives.*

32. King, "Labor's Aphasia." See also King, *Black Shoals.*

33. US Department of Health and Human Services, Administration for Children and Families, "Programs to Reduce Human Trafficking."

34. Rescue and Restore Regional Grant Program, Department of Health and Human Services, https://www.homelandsecuritygrants.info/Grant-Details/gid/20093. "Each Rescue and Restore Regional partner oversees and builds the capacity of a local anti-trafficking network to better identify and work with victims, encouraging a cohesive and collaborative approach." US Department of Health and Human Services, Administration for Children and Families, Office of Refugee Resettlement, "Anti-Trafficking in Persons Programs.

35. US Department of Health and Human Services, Administration for Children and Families, "Testimony on ACF Activities."

36. US Department of Health and Human Services, Administration for Children and Families, "Testimony on ACF Activities."

37. Razack, "Domestic Violence."

38. See Clough and Willse, *Beyond Biopolitics*.

39. Moore, *Legal Spectatorship*.

40. "Hidden in Plain Sight"; and Hartman, "Anarchy of Colored Girls."

41. Gustafson analyzes welfare fraud hotlines managed by counties that provide "bounties" for reporting supposed fraud or suspicious activity. These resulted in "degradation ceremonies" where Black communities were required to endure bodily testing to animate their personhood and worth in order to be a recipient of services and resources. An "allure" is produced that goes far beyond the scope of these programs and establishes terms of racial inferiority. Gustafson, "Degradation Ceremonies."

42. US Department of Health and Human Services, Administration for Children and Families, Office of Refugee Resettlement, "Anti-Trafficking in Persons Programs."

43. Hua, *Trafficking Women's Human Rights*.

44. Fukushima, *Migrant Crossings*.

45. African American Policy Forum, "Statement on Tioni Theus."

46. Martin and Hill, "Debunking the Myth."

47. Volpp, "Citizen and the Terrorist"; Naber, "'Look'"; and Naber, *Arab America*. For a discussion of the sexuality and neoliberal securitization in "human-security states," see Amar, *Security Archipelago*. For a discussion of militarized humanitarianism, the geopolitics of gender violence, and Western imperialisms, see Abu-Lughod et al., *Cunning of Gender Violence*.

CONCLUSION

1. Davis et al., *Abolition. Feminism. Now*, 4.

2. Spade and Willse, "Gay Hate Crimes Activism"; and Reddy, *Freedom with Violence*.

3. Hong, *Death Beyond Disavowal*; and Hong, "Intersectionality and Incommensurability."

4. Shim, "Beyond #StopAsianHate."

5. Hwang, "Bad Apples."

6. Hwang, "Bad Apples."

7. Gehi and Munshi, "Connecting State Violence."

8. Rodríguez, "'Asian Exception'"; and C. Kim, *Asian Americans*.

9. Gilmore, "In the Shadow." Gilmore argues that the "anti-state state" rebuilds the state and its form. Gilmore, *Abolition Geography*, 487.

10. Tuck and Yang, "What Justice Wants."

11. Best and Hartman, "Fugitive Justice."

Bibliography

Abdulhadi, Rabab, Evelyn Alsultany, and Nadine Christine Naber, eds. *Arab and Arab American Feminisms: Gender, Violence, and Belonging.* Syracuse University Press, 2011.

Abrego, Leisy J. *Sacrificing Families: Navigating Laws, Labor, and Love Across Borders.* Stanford University Press, 2014.

Abrego, Leisy, Mat Coleman, Daniel E. Martínez, Cecilia Menjívar, and Jeremy Slack. "Making Immigrants into Criminals: Legal Processes of Criminalization in the Post-IIRIRA Era." *Journal on Migration and Human Security* 5, no. 3 (2017): 694–714.

Abrego, Leisy J., and Sarah M. Lakhani. "Incomplete Inclusion: Legal Violence and Immigrants in Liminal Legal Statuses." *Law and Policy* 37, no. 4 (2015): 265–93.

Abrego, Leisy J., and Genevieve Negrón-Gonzales, eds. *We Are Not Dreamers: Undocumented Scholars Theorize Undocumented Life in the United States.* Duke University Press, 2020.

Abu-Lughod, Lila. "Can There Be a Feminist Ethnography?" *Women and Performance: A Journal of Feminist Theory* 5, no. 1 (1988): 7–27.

Abu-Lughod, Lila. "Do Muslim Women Really Need Saving? Anthropological Reflections on Cultural Relativism and Its Others." *American Anthropologist* 104, no. 3 (2002): 783–90.

Abu-Lughod, Lila, Rema Hammami, and Nādirah Shalhūb-Kīfūrkiyān, eds. *The Cunning of Gender Violence: Geopolitics and Feminism.* Duke University Press, 2023.

African American Policy Forum. "AAPF Statement on Tioni Theus, Human Trafficking, and Super Bowl LVI." February 12, 2022. https://www.aapf.org/post/aapf-statement -tioni-theus-super-bowl.

American Civil Liberties Union. "Prison Rape Elimination Act of 2003 (PREA)." April 29, 2011. https://www.aclu.org/documents/prison-rape-elimination-act-2003-prea.

Amar, Paul. *The Security Archipelago: Human-Security States, Sexuality Politics, and the End of Neoliberalism.* Duke University Press, 2013.

Amireh, Amal. "Palestinian Women's Disappearing Act: The Suicide Bomber Through Western Feminist Eyes." In *Arab and Arab American Feminisms: Gender Violence and*

Belonging, edited by Rabab Abdulhadi, Evelyn Alsultany, and Nadine C. Naber. Syracuse University Press, 2011.

Amnesty International. *Maze of Injustice: The Failure to Protect Indigenous Women from Sexual Violence in the USA*. Amnesty International, 2007.

Arvin, Maile, Eve Tuck, and Angie Morrill. "Decolonizing Feminism: Challenging Connections Between Settler Colonialism and Heteropatriarchy." *Feminist Formations* 25, no. 1 (2013): 8–34.

Battered Immigrant Women Protection Act of 1999. 2nd ed. US Government Printing Office, 2000.

Battered Immigrant Women Protection Act of 1999, Pub. L. No. 106-386, tit. V, § 1501, 114 Stat. 1518 (2000).

Ben-Moshe, Liat. *Decarcerating Disability: Deinstitutionalization and Prison Abolition*. University of Minnesota Press, 2020.

Bernstein, Elizabeth. *Brokered Subjects: Sex, Trafficking, and the Politics of Freedom*. University of Chicago Press, 2018.

Bernstein, Elizabeth. "Militarized Humanitarianism Meets Carceral Feminism: The Politics of Sex, Rights, and Freedom in Contemporary Antitrafficking Campaigns." *Signs: Journal of Women in Culture and Society* 36, no. 1 (2010): 45–71.

Bernstein, Elizabeth. "The Sexual Politics of the 'New Abolitionism.'" *Differences* 18, no. 3 (2007): 128–51.

Bernstein, Elizabeth. *Temporarily Yours: Intimacy, Authenticity, and the Commerce of Sex*. University of Chicago Press, 2007.

Best, Stephen, and Saidiya Hartman. "Fugitive Justice." *Representations*, no. 92 (2005): 1–15.

Beutin, Lyndsey P. *Trafficking in Antiblackness: Modern-Day Slavery, White Indemnity, and Racial Justice*. Duke University Press, 2023.

Bhattacharjee, Anannya. "Private Fists and Public Force: Race, Gender, and Surveillance." In *Policing the National Body: Race, Gender, and Criminalization*, edited by Jael Miriam Silliman and Anannya Bhattacharjee. South End, 2002.

Bhuyan, Rupaleem. "The Production of the 'Battered Immigrant' in Public Policy and Domestic Violence Advocacy." *Journal of Interpersonal Violence* 23, no. 2 (2008): 153–70.

Bierria, Alisa. "Missing in Action: Violence, Power, and Discerning Agency." *Hypatia* 29, no. 1 (2014): 129–45.

Bierria, Alisa, Jakeya Caruthers, and Brooke Lober. Introduction to *Abolition Feminisms*, vol. 2, *Feminist Ruptures Against the Carceral State*, edited by Alisa Bierria, Jakeya Caruthers, and Brooke Lober. Haymarket, 2002.

Bierria, Alisa, Jakeya Caruthers, and Brooke Lober, eds. *Abolition Feminisms*. Vol. 2, *Feminist Ruptures Against the Carceral State*. Haymarket, 2022.

Bierria, Alisa, and Colby Lenz. "Battering Court Syndrome: A Structural Critique of 'Failure to Protect.'" In *The Politicization of Safety*, edited by Jane Stoever. NYU Press, 2019.

Bierria, Alisa, and Colby Lenz. *Defending Self-Defense: A Call to Action*. Survived and Punished, 2022.

"Black Introduces U Visa Reform Act." Press Release. http://black.house.gov/press
-release/black-introduces-u-visa-reform-act. Accessed May 5, 2025.

Bracke, Sarah. "From 'Saving Women' to 'Saving Gays': Rescue Narratives and Their
Dis/Continuities." *European Journal of Women's Studies* 19, no. 2 (2012): 237–52.

Brown, Wendy. *States of Injury: Power and Freedom in Late Modernity*. Princeton University Press, 1995.

Budd, Kristin M. "Incarcerated Women and Girls." The Sentencing Project, July 24,
2024. https://www.sentencingproject.org/fact-sheet/incarcerated-women-and
-girls/.

Bumiller, Kristin. *In an Abusive State: How Neoliberalism Appropriated the Feminist
Movement Against Sexual Violence*. Duke University Press, 2008.

Capps, Randy, Michael Fix, and Jie Zong. *A Profile of U.S. Children with Unauthorized
Immigrant Parents*. Migration Policy Institute, 2016.

Capps, Randy, Marc Rosenblum, Cristina Rodríguez, and Muzaffar Chishti. *Delegation
and Divergence: A Study of 287(g) State and Local Immigration Enforcement*. Migration Policy Institute, 2011.

Carson, Grace. "Tribal Sovereignty, Decolonization, and Abolition: Why Tribes Should
Reconsider Punishment." *UCLA Law Review* 69 (2022): 1077–1128.

Chacón, Jennifer M. "Managing Migration Through Crime." *Columbia Law Review
Sidebar* 109 (2009): 135–48.

Chacón, Jennifer M. "Producing Liminal Legality." *Denver University Law Review* 92,
no. 4 (2015): 709–67.

Chacón, Jennifer M. "Tensions and Trade-Offs: Protecting Trafficking Victims in the
Era of Immigration Enforcement." *University of Pennsylvania Law Review* 158, no. 6
(2010): 1609–53.

Chávez, Karma R. *Queer Migration Politics: Activist Rhetoric and Coalitional Possibilities*.
University of Illinois Press, 2013.

Cházaro, Angélica. "Challenging the 'Criminal Alien' Paradigm." *UCLA Law Review* 63
(2016): 594–664.

Chen, C.-I., Dulani, J., and L. L. Piepzna-Samarasinha. *The Revolution Starts at Home:
Confronting Intimate Violence Within Activist Communities*. AK Press, 2016.

Clough, Patricia Ticineto, and Craig Willse. *Beyond Biopolitics: Essays on the Governance
of Life and Death*. Duke University Press, 2011.

Comrie, Nazmia E. A., and Faye Elkins. *Reducing Crime by Increasing Trust in an Immigrant Community*. US Government Printing Office, 2013.

Constable, Marianne. *Just Silences: The Limits and Possibilities of Modern Law*. Princeton
University Press, 2005.

Constable, Marianne. *Our Word Is Our Bond: How Legal Speech Acts*. Stanford University Press, 2014.

Coutin, Susan Bibler. *Exiled Home: Salvadoran Transnational Youth in the Aftermath of
Violence*. Duke University Press, 2016.

Coutin, Susan Bibler. *Legalizing Moves: Salvadoran Immigrants' Struggle for U.S. Residency*. University of Michigan Press, 2000.

Cover, Robert M. *Narrative, Violence, and the Law: The Essays of Robert Cover*. Edited by Martha Minow, Michael Ryan, and Austin Sarat. University of Michigan Press, 1995.

Crenshaw, Kimberlé. "Demarginalizing the Intersection of Race and Sex: A Black Feminist Critique of Antidiscrimination Doctrine, Feminist Theory and Antiracist Politics." *University of Chicago Legal Forum* 1989, no. 1: 139–67.

Crenshaw, Kimberlé. "Mapping the Margins: Intersectionality, Identity Politics, and Violence Against Women of Color." *Stanford Law Review* 43, no. 6 (1991): 1241–99.

Dahlstrom, Julie. "Trafficking and the Shallow State." *UC Irvine Law Review* 12, no. 1 (2021): 61–110.

Darian-Smith, Eve. "Ethnographies of Law." In *The Blackwell Companion to Law and Society*, edited by Austin Sarat. Blackwell, 2004.

Dasgupta, Shamita Das, and Patricia Eng. *Safety and Justice for All: Examining the Relationship Between the Women's Anti-Violence Movement and the Criminal Legal System*. Ms. Foundation for Women, 2003.

Davis, Angela Y. *Abolition Democracy: Beyond Empire, Prisons, and Torture*. Seven Stories, 2005.

Davis, Angela Y. *Are Prisons Obsolete?* Seven Stories, 2003.

Davis, Angela Y. "Race and Criminalization." In *The House That Race Built: Black Americans, U.S. Terrain*, edited by Wahneema Lubiano. Random House, 1997.

Davis, Angela Y., Gina Dent, Erica R. Meiners, and Beth Richie. *Abolition. Feminism. Now.* Haymarket Books, 2022.

Davis, Angela Y., and Cassandra Shaylor. "Race, Gender, and the Prison Industrial Complex: California and Beyond." *Meridians* 2, no. 1 (2001): 1–25.

Dayan, Colin. *The Law Is a White Dog: How Legal Rituals Make and Unmake Persons*. Princeton University Press, 2011.

Deer, Sarah. *The Beginning and End of Rape: Confronting Sexual Violence in Native America*. University of Minnesota Press, 2015.

Deer, Sarah. "Decolonizing Rape Law: A Native Feminist Synthesis of Safety and Sovereignty." *Wičazo Ša Review* 24, no. 2 (2009): 149–67.

Deer, Sarah. "Relocation Revisited: Sex Trafficking of Native Women in the United States." *Mitchell Hamline Law Review* 36, no. 2 (2010): 621–83.

Dholakia, Nazish. "Women's Incarceration Rates Are Skyrocketing. These Advocates Are Trying to Change That." Vera, May 17, 2021. https://www.vera.org/news/womens-incarceration-rates-are-skyrocketing.

Dixon, Ejeris, and Leah Lakshmi Piepzna-Samarasinha, eds. *Beyond Survival: Strategies and Stories from the Transformative Justice Movement*. AK Press, 2020.

Dubrofsky, Rachel E., and Shoshana Magnet. *Feminist Surveillance Studies*. Duke University Press, 2015.

Elia, Nada, Jodi Kim, Shana L. Redmond, Dylan Rodríguez, Sarita Echavez See, and David Hernández, eds. *Critical Ethnic Studies: A Reader*. Duke University Press, 2016.

Escobar, Martha D. *Captivity Beyond Prisons: Criminalization Experiences of Latina (Im)Migrants*. University of Texas Press, 2016.

Esmeir, Samera. *Juridical Humanity: A Colonial History*. Stanford University Press, 2012.

Farley, Anthony Paul. "Accumulation." *Michigan Journal of Race and Law* 11 (2005): 51–73.

Fellows, Mary Louise, and Sherene Razack. "The Race to Innocence: Confronting Hierarchical Relations Among Women." *Journal of Gender, Race and Justice* 1 (1998): 335–52.

Ferreira da Silva, Denise. *Toward a Global Idea of Race*. University of Minnesota Press, 2007.

Ferreira da Silva, Denise. "Towards a Critique of the Socio-Logos of Justice: The Analytics of Raciality and the Production of Universality." *Social Identities* 7 (2001): 421–54.

Finklea, Kristin. "Trafficking in Persons: Grants for Victim Services in the United States." Report No. R47466. Congressional Research Service, 2023.

Finley, Chris. "Ghostly Care: Boarding Schools, Prisons, and Debt in Rhymes for Young Ghouls." In *Abolition Feminisms Volume 1: Organizing, Survival, and Transformative Practice, Edited by Alisa Bierria, Jakeya Caruthers, and Brooke Lober*. Haymarket Press, 2022.

Fortuny, Karina, and Ajay Chaudry. *Overview of Immigrants' Eligibility for SNAP, TANF, Medicaid, and CHIP*. Urban Institute. 2012.

Fujiwara, Lynn. *Mothers Without Citizenship: Asian Immigrant Families and the Consequences of Welfare Reform*. University of Minnesota Press, 2008.

Fukushima, Annie Isabel. *Migrant Crossings: Witnessing Human Trafficking in the U.S.* Stanford University Press, 2019.

Garcia, Romina. "'All Canned Foods Are Expired but Still Edible': A Critique of Anti-Violence Advocacy and the Perpetuation of Antiblackness." In *Abolition Feminisms*, vol. 2, *Feminist Ruptures Against the Carceral State*, edited by Alisa Bierria, Jakeya Caruthers, and Brooke Lober. Haymarket Books, 2022.

Gehi, Pooja, and Soniya Munshi. "Connecting State Violence and Anti-Violence: An Examination of the Impact of VAWA and Hate Crimes Legislation on Asian American Communities." *Asian American Law Journal* 21 (2014): 5–42.

Georgis, Dina. *The Better Story: Queer Affects from the Middle East*. SUNY Press, 2013.

Gilmore, Ruth Wilson. "Abolition Geography and the Problem of Innocence." In *Futures of Black Radicalism*, edited by Gaye Theresa Johnson and Alex Lubin. Verso, 2017.

Gilmore, Ruth Wilson. *Abolition Geography: Essays Towards Liberation*. Edited by Brenna Bhandar and Alberto Toscano. Verso, 2022.

Gilmore, Ruth Wilson. "In the Shadow of the Shadow State." *Scholar and Feminist Online* 12, no. 2 (2016). https://sfonline.barnard.edu/ruth-wilson-gilmore-in-the-shadow-of-the-shadow-state/.

Goodmark, Leigh. *Imperfect Victims: Criminalized Survivors and the Promise of Abolition Feminism*. University of California Press, 2023.

Goodmark, Leigh. *A Troubled Marriage: Domestic Violence and the Legal System*. NYU Press, 2012.

Gottschalk, Marie. *The Prison and the Gallows: The Politics of Mass Incarceration in America*. Cambridge University Press, 2006.

Gustafson, Kaaryn S. *Cheating Welfare: Public Assistance and the Criminalization of Poverty*. NYU Press, 2011.

Gustafson, Kaaryn S. "Degradation Ceremonies and the Criminalization of Low-Income Women." *UC Irvine Law Review* 3 (2013): 297–358.

Haley, Sarah. "Flesh Work and the Reproduction of Black Culpability." In *Antiblackness*, edited by João H. Costa Vargas and Moon-Kie Jung. Duke University Press, 2021.

Hallett, Miranda Cady. "Temporary Protection, Enduring Contradiction: The Contested and Contradictory Meanings of Temporary Immigration Status." *Law and Social Inquiry* 39, no. 3 (2014): 621–42.

Han, Sora Y. *Letters of the Law: Race and the Fantasy of Colorblindness in American Law*. Stanford Law Books, 2015.

Han, Sora Y. "The Politics of Race in Asian American Jurisprudence." *UCLA Asian Pacific American Law Journal* 11, no. 1 (2006): 1–40.

Hanhardt, Christina B. *Safe Space: Gay Neighborhood History and the Politics of Violence*. Duke University Press, 2013.

Hanson, Emily, and Lisa Sacco. "The Violence Against Women Act (VAWA) Reauthorization: Issues for Congress." Report No. R46742. Congressional Research Service, 2021.

Harcourt, Bernard E. *Illusion of Order: The False Promise of Broken Windows Policing*. Harvard University Press, 2001.

Haritaworn, Jin, Adi Kuntsman, and Silvia Posocco. "Murderous Inclusions." *International Feminist Journal of Politics* 15, no. 4 (2013): 445–52.

Haritaworn, Jin, Ghaida Moussa, and Syrus Marcus Ware. *Marvellous Grounds: Queer of Colour Formations in Toronto*. Between the Lines, 2018.

Harris, Cheryl I. "Whiteness as Property." *Harvard Law Review* 106, no. 8 (1993): 1707–91.

Hartman, Saidiya. "The Anarchy of Colored Girls Assembled in a Riotous Manner." *South Atlantic Quarterly* 117, no. 3 (2018) 465–90.

Hartman, Saidiya V. *Scenes of Subjection: Terror, Slavery, and Self-Making in Nineteenth-Century America*. Oxford University Press, 1997.

Hartman, Saidiya. "Venus in Two Acts." *Small Axe: A Journal of Criticism* 12, no. 2 (2008): 1–14.

Hemmings, Clare. *Why Stories Matter: The Political Grammar of Feminist Theory*. Duke University Press, 2011.

Herman, Susan, David R. Anderson, Diane Johnson, Karen Dempsey, David Weisburd, Rosann Greenspan, Graham Farrell, and Justin Ready. *Bringing Victims into Community Policing*, National Center for Victims of Crime and the Police Foundation. US Department of Justice, Office of Community Oriented Policing Services, 2002. https://www.ojp.gov/ncjrs/virtual-library/abstracts/bringing-victims-community-policing. US Government Printing Office.

Hernández, Kelly Lytle. *City of Inmates: Conquest, Rebellion, and the Rise of Human Caging in Los Angeles, 1771–1965*. University of North Carolina Press, 2017.

"Hidden in Plain Sight: ICE's Work to Combat Human Trafficking." US Department of Homeland Security, last modified January 11, 2013. https://www.dhs.gov/archive/news/2013/01/11/hidden-plain-sight.

Hill, Annie. "The Rhetoric of Modern-Day Slavery: Analogical Links and Historical Kinks in the United Kingdom's Anti-Trafficking Plan." *Philosophia* 7, no. 2 (2017): 241–60.

Hinton, Elizabeth Kai. *From the War on Poverty to the War on Crime: The Making of Mass Incarceration in America*. Harvard University Press, 2016.

Hong, Grace Kyungwon. *Death Beyond Disavowal: The Impossible Politics of Difference*. University of Minnesota Press, 2015.

Hong, Grace Kyungwon. "Intersectionality and Incommensurability: Third World Feminism and Asian Decolonization." In *Asian American Feminisms and Women of Color Politics*, edited by Lynn Fujiwara and Shireen Roshanravan. University of Washington Press, 2018.

Hua, Julietta. *Trafficking Women's Human Rights*. University of Minnesota Press, 2011.

Hunt, Sarah. "Representing Colonial Violence: Trafficking, Sex Work, and the Violence of Law." *Atlantis: Critical Studies in Gender, Culture, and Social Justice* 37, no. 2 (2015): 25–39.

Hwang, Ren-yo. "Bad Apples, Rotted Roots, and the Three Rs of Reformist Reforms." In *Abolition Feminisms*, vol. 2, *Feminist Ruptures Against the Carceral State*, edited by Alisa Bierria, Jakeya Caruthers, and Brooke Lober. Haymarket Books, 2022.

INCITE! Women of Color Against Violence. *Color of Violence: The INCITE! Anthology*. South End, 2006.

INCITE! Women of Color Against Violence. *The Revolution Will Not Be Funded: Beyond the Non-Profit Industrial Complex*. South End, 2007.

INCITE! and Critical Resistance. "Critical Resistance-Incite! Statement on Gender Violence and the Prison-Industrial Complex." *Crime and Social Justice* 30, no. 3 (2003): 141–50.

Ivie, Stacey, and Natalie Nanasi. "The U Visa: An Effective Resource for Law Enforcement." *FBI Law Enforcement Bulletin* 78, no. 10 (2009): 10–16.

Jaleel, Rana M. *The Work of Rape*. Duke University Press, 2021.

Jamal, Amaney, and Nadine Naber, eds. *Race and Arab Americans Before and After 9/11: From Invisible Citizens to Visible Subjects*. Syracuse University Press, 2008.

Kaba, Mariame, and Shira Hassan. *Fumbling Towards Repair: A Workbook for Community Accountability Facilitators*. Project NIA, 2019.

Kaguyutan, Janice, Leslye Orloff, and Negar Ashtari. "The Violence Against Women Act of 1994 and 2000: Immigration Protections for Battered Immigrants." *Domestic Violence Report* 6, no. 3 (2001): 33–48.

Kamhi, Alison, and Sarah Lakhani. *A Guide to State Laws on U Visa and T Visa Certifications*. Immigrant Legal Resource Center, 2020.

Kandaswamy, Priya. *Domestic Contradictions: Race and Gendered Citizenship from Reconstruction to Welfare Reform*. Duke University Press, 2021.

Kang, Laura Hyun Yi. *Compositional Subjects: Enfiguring Asian/American Women*. Duke University Press, 2002.

Kang, Laura Hyun Yi. *Traffic in Asian Women*. Duke University Press, 2020.

Kempadoo, Kamala, and Jo Doezema. *Global Sex Workers: Rights, Resistance, and Redefinition*. Routledge, 1998.

Kempadoo, Kamala, Jyoti Sanghera, and Bandana Pattanaik. *Trafficking and Prostitution Reconsidered: New Perspectives on Migration, Sex Work, and Human Rights*. Paradigm, 2005.

Kemper, Nathan. *The 2022 Violence Against Women Act Reauthorization*. Report No. R47570. Congressional Research Service, 2023.

Kemper, Nathan, and Lisa Sacco. *The Violence Against Women Act (VAWA): Historical Overview, Funding, and Reauthorization*. Report No. R45410. Congressional Research Service, 2019.

Kerwin, Donald. "From IIRIRA to Trump: Connecting the Dots to the Current US Immigration Policy Crisis." *Journal on Migration and Human Security* 6, no. 3 (2018): 192–204.

Kim, Claire Jean. *Asian Americans in an Anti-Black World*. Cambridge University Press, 2023.

Kim, Mimi E. "The Carceral Creep: Gender-Based Violence, Race, and the Expansion of the Punitive State, 1973–1983." *Social Problems* 67, no. 2 (2020): 251–69.

Kim, Mimi. "From Carceral Feminism to Transformative Justice: Women-of-Color Feminism and Alternatives to Incarceration." *Journal of Ethnic and Cultural Diversity in Social Work* 27, no. 3 (2018): 219–33.

Kim, Mimi, Morgan Bassichis, Felipe Hernandez, RJ Maccani, Gaurav Jashnani, Bench Ansfield, Jenna Peters-Golden, and Molly Porzig. "A World Without Walls: Stopping Harm and Abolishing the Prison Industrial Complex." *Abolitionist*, no. 16 (2012): 5–6.

Kim, Mimi E., Cameron Rasmussen, Durrell M. Washington, and Mariame Kaba, eds. *Abolition and Social Work: Possibilities, Paradoxes, and the Practice of Community Care*. Haymarket Books, 2024.

King, Tiffany Lethabo. *The Black Shoals: Offshore Formations of Black and Native Studies*. Duke University Press, 2019.

King, Tiffany. "Labor's Aphasia: Toward Antiblackness as Constitutive to Settler Colonialism." *Decolonization: Indigeneity, Education and Society*, June 10, 2014. https://decolonization.wordpress.com/2014/06/10/labors-aphasia-toward-antiblackness-as-constitutive-to-settler-colonialism/.

Kolker, Abigail F. *The 287(g) Program: State and Local Immigration Enforcement*. Report No. RIF11898. Congressional Research Service, 2021.

Komar, Liz, Alexandra Bailey, Clarissa Gonzalez, Elizabeth Isaacs, Kate Mogulescu, and Monica Szlekovics. *Sentencing Reform for Criminalized Survivors: Learning from New York's Domestic Violence Survivors Justice Act*. Sentencing Project, 2023.

Koyama, Emi. "Disloyal to Feminism: Abuse of Survivors Within the Domestic Violence Shelter System." In *Color of Violence: The INCITE! Anthology*. South End, 2006.

Kwong, Deanna. "Removing Barriers for Battered Immigrant Women: A Comparison of Immigrant Protections Under VAWA I and II." *Berkeley Women's Law Journal*, 17 (2002): 137–52.

Lindsley, Syd. "The Gendered Assault on Immigrants." In *Policing the National Body: Sex, Race, and Criminalization*, edited by Jael Silliman and Anannya Bhattacharjee. South End, 2002.

Luibhéid, Eithne. *Entry Denied: Controlling Sexuality at the Border*. University of Minnesota Press, 2002.

Luibhéid, Eithne, and Karma R. Chávez, eds. *Queer and Trans Migrations: Dynamics of Illegalization, Detention, and Deportation*. University of Illinois Press, 2021.

Macías-Rojas, Patrisia. *From Deportation to Prison: The Politics of Immigration Enforcement in Post–Civil Rights America*. NYU Press, 2016.

Macías-Rojas, Patrisia. "Immigration and the War on Crime: Law and Order Politics and the Illegal Immigration Reform and Immigrant Responsibility Act of 1996." *Journal on Migration and Human Security* 6, no. 1 (2018): 1–25.

Mahoney, Amanda. "How Failure to Protect Laws Punish the Vulnerable." *Health Matrix: The Journal of Law-Medicine* 29, no. 1 (2019): 429–61.

Maira, Sunaina. "'Good' and 'Bad' Muslim Citizens: Feminists, Terrorists, and U.S. Orientalisms." *Feminist Studies* 35, no. 3 (2009): 631–56.

Martin, Lauren, and Annie Hill. "Debunking the Myth of 'Super Bowl Sex Trafficking': Media Hype or Evidence-Based Coverage." *Anti-Trafficking Review*, no. 1 (2019): 13–29.

Matsuda, Mari J. *Where Is Your Body? And Other Essays on Race, Gender, and the Law*. Beacon, 1996.

Maynard, Robyn. "#Blacksexworkerslivesmatter: White-Washed 'Anti-Slavery' and the Appropriation of Black Suffering." *Feminist Wire*, September 9, 2015. https://thefeministwire.com/2015/09/blacksexworkerslivesmatter-white-washed-anti-slavery-and-the-appropriation-of-black-suffering/.

Maynard, Robyn. *Policing Black Lives: State Violence in Canada from Slavery to the Present*. Fernwood, 2017.

Melamed, Jodi. *Represent and Destroy: Rationalizing Violence in the New Racial Capitalism*. University of Minnesota Press, 2011.

Melamed, Jodi, and Chandan Reddy. "Using Liberal Rights to Enforce Racial Capitalism." *Insights from Social Sciences*, July 30, 2019. https://items.ssrc.org/race-capitalism/using-liberal-rights-to-enforce-racial-capitalism/.

Mijente, the National Immigration Project, the Immigrant Defense Project, and Empower LLC. *Who's Behind ICE? The Tech and Data Companies Fueling Deportations*. 2018. https://mijente.net/wp-content/uploads/2018/10/WHO%E2%80%99S-BEHIND-ICE_-The-Tech-and-Data-Companies-Fueling-Deportations-_v1.pdf.

Million, Dian. *Therapeutic Nations: Healing in an Age of Indigenous Human Rights*. University of Arizona Press, 2013.

Mogul, Joey L., Andrea J. Ritchie, and Kay Whitlock. *Queer (In)Justice: The Criminalization of LGBT People in the United States*. Beacon, 2011.

Moore, Kelli. *Legal Spectatorship: Slavery and the Visual Culture of Domestic Violence*. Duke University Press, 2022.

Moreton-Robinson, Aileen. *Talkin' Up to the White Woman: Aboriginal Women and Feminism*. Queensland University Press, 2000.

Motomura, Hiroshi. *Immigration Outside the Law*. Oxford University Press, 2014.

Munshi, Soniya. "Multiplicities of Violence: Responses to September 11 from South Asian Women's Organizations." *Race/Ethnicity: Multidisciplinary Global Contexts* 4, no. 3 (2011): 419–36.

Naber, Nadine C. *Arab America: Gender, Cultural Politics, and Activism*. NYU Press, 2012.

Naber, Nadine C. "Decolonizing Culture: Beyond Orientalist and Anti-Orientalist Feminisms." In *Arab and Arab American Feminisms: Gender, Violence and Belonging*, edited by Rabab Abdulhadi, Evelyn Alsultany, and Nadine Naber. Syracuse University Press, 2011.

Naber, Nadine C. "'Look, Mohammed the Terrorist Is Coming!': Cultural Racism, Nation-Based Racism, and the Intersectionality of Oppressions After 9/11." In *Race and Arab Americans Before and After 9/11: From Invisible Citizens to Visible Subjects*, edited by Jamal Amaney and Nadine C. Naber. Syracuse University Press, 2008.

Naber, Nadine C. "So Our History Doesn't Become Your Future: The Local and Global Politics of Coalition Building Post September 11th." *Journal of Asian American Studies* 5, no. 3 (2002): 217–42.

Naimou, Angela. *Salvage Work: U.S. and Caribbean Literatures amid the Debris of Legal Personhood*. Fordham University Press, 2015.

Narayan, Kirin. "Ethnography and Fiction: Where Is the Border?" *Anthropology and Humanism* 24, no. 2 (1999): 134–47.

Ocen, Priscilla A. "The New Racially Restrictive Covenant: Race, Welfare, and the Policing of Black Women in Subsidized Housing." *UCLA Law Review* 59, no. 6 (2012): 1542–82.

Ocen, Priscilla A. "Punishing Pregnancy: Race, Incarceration, and the Shackling of Pregnant Prisoners." *California Law Review* 100, no. 5 (2012): 1239–311.

Ocen, Priscilla A. "Unshackling Intersectionality." *Du Bois Review: Social Science Research on Race* 10, no. 2 (2013): 471–83.

Oparah, Chinyere [Julia Sudbury]. *Global Lockdown: Race, Gender, and the Prison-Industrial Complex*. Routledge, 2005.

Oparah, Chinyere [Julia Sudbury]. "Rethinking Antiviolence Strategies: Lessons from Black Women's Movement in Britain." In *Color of Violence: The INCITE! Anthology*, edited by INCITE! South End, 2006.

Orloff, Leslye E., Kathryn Isom, and Edmondo Saballos. "Mandatory U-Visa Certification Unnecessarily Undermines the Purpose of the Violence Against Women Act's Immigration Protections and It's 'Any Credible Evidence' Rules—a Call for Consistency." *Georgetown Journal of Gender and the Law* 11, no. 2 (2010): 619–48.

Orloff, Leslye, and Janice Kaguyutan. "Offering a Helping Hand: Legal Protections for Battered Immigrant Women: A History of Legislative Responses." *Journal of Gender, Social Policy and the Law* 10, no. 1 (2001): 95–183.

Paik, A. Naomi. *Bans, Walls, Raids, Sanctuary: Understanding U.S. Immigration for the Twenty-First Century*. University of California Press, 2020.

Park, Lisa Sun-Hee. "Challenging Public Charge Policy: Coalitional Immigrant Community Strategies." *Journal of Asian American Studies* 13, no. 3 (2010): 371–87.

Perreira, Krista M., and Juan M. Pedroza. "Policies of Exclusion: Implications for the Health of Immigrants and Their Children." *Annual Review of Public Health* 40 (2019): 147–66.

Piepzna-Samarasinha, Leah Lakshmi. *Care Work: Dreaming Disability Justice*. Arsenal Pulp, 2018.

Prah, Pamela. "Domestic Violence." *CQ Researcher* 16, no. 1 (2006): 1–49.

Razack, Sherene. "Domestic Violence as Gender Persecution: Policing the Borders of

Nation, Race, and Gender." *Canadian Journal of Women and the Law* 8, no. 1 (1995): 45–88.

Razack, Sherene. "'Simple Logic': Race, the Identity Documents Rule, and the Story of a Nation Besieged and Betrayed." In *Crossroads, Directions, and a New Critical Race Theory*, edited by Francisco Valdes, Jerome McCristal Culp, and Angela P. Harris. Temple University Press, 2002.

Reddy, Chandan. *Freedom with Violence: Race, Sexuality, and the US State*. Duke University Press, 2011.

"Rescue and Restore Victims of Human Trafficking Regional Program." US Department of Homeland Security Grants Info. Accessed January 2024. https://www.homeland securitygrants.info/GrantDetails.aspx?gid=20093.

Richie, Beth. *Arrested Justice: Black Women, Violence, and America's Prison Nation*. NYU Press, 2012.

Richie, Beth. "Reimagining the Movement to End Gender Violence: Anti-Racism, Prison Abolition, Women of Color Feminisms, and Other Radical Visions of Justice." *University of Miami Race and Social Justice Law Review* 257, no. 5 (2015): 257–73.

Richie, Beth, Valli Kalei Kanuha, and Kayla Marie Martensen. "Colluding with and Resisting the State: Organizing Against Gender Violence in the U.S." *Feminist Criminology* 16, no. 3 (2021): 247–65.

Ritchie, Andrea J. *Invisible No More: Police Violence Against Black Women and Women of Color*. Beacon, 2017.

Ritchie, Andrea J. "Law Enforcement Violence Against Women of Color." In *Law Enforcement Violence against Women of Color*. South End, 2006.

Ritchie, Andrea J., and Delores Jones-Brown. "Policing Race, Gender, and Sex: A Review of Law Enforcement Policies." *Women and Criminal Justice* 27, no. 1 (2017): 21–50.

Roberts, Dorothy E. *Killing the Black Body: Race, Reproduction, and the Meaning of Liberty*. Pantheon Books, 1997.

Roberts, Dorothy E. *Shattered Bonds: The Color of Child Welfare*. Basic Books, 2002.

Rodríguez, Dylan. "Asian American Studies in the Age of the Prison Industrial Complex: Departures and Re-Narrations." *Review of Education, Pedagogy, Cultural Studies* 27, no. 3 (2005): 241–63.

Rodríguez, Dylan. "The 'Asian Exception' and the Scramble for Legibility: Toward an Abolitionist Approach to Anti-Asian Violence." *Society and Space*, April 8, 2021.

Rojas, Clarissa, Mimi Kim, and Alicia Bierria. "Community Accountability: Emerging Movements to Transform Violence." *Social Justice* 37, no. 4 (122) (2011): 1–11.

Scott, Joan W. "The Evidence of Experience." *Critical Inquiry* 17, no. 4 (1991): 773–97.

Shih, Elena. "The Fantasy of Spotting Human Trafficking: Training Spectacles in Racist Surveillance." *Wagadu: A Journal of Transnational Women's and Gender Studies* 22, no. 1 (2021): 105–37.

Shih, Elena. *Manufacturing Freedom: Sex Work, Anti-Trafficking Rehab, and the Racial Wages of Rescue*. University of California Press, 2023.

Shim, Hyejin. "Beyond #StopAsianHate: Criminalization, Gender, and Asian Abolition Feminism." In *Abolition Feminisms*, vol. 2, *Feminist Ruptures Against the Carceral State*, edited by Alisa Bierria, Jakeya Caruthers, and Brooke Lober. Haymarket Books, 2022.

Silliman, Jael M., and Anannya Bhattacharjee, eds. *Policing the National Body: Race, Gender and Criminalization in the United States*. South End, 2002.

Simon, Jonathan. *Governing Through Crime: How the War on Crime Transformed American Democracy and Created a Culture of Fear*. Oxford University Press, 2007.

Simpson, Audra. "On Ethnographic Refusal: Indigeneity, 'Voice' and Colonial Citizenship." *Junctures: The Journal for Thematic Dialogue* 9, no. 71 (2007): 191–215.

Smith, Linda Tuhiwai. *Decolonizing Methodologies: Research and Indigenous Peoples*. St. Martin's, 1999.

Smith, Nat, and Eric A. Stanley. *Captive Genders: Trans Embodiment and the Prison Industrial Complex*. AK Press, 2011.

Sokoloff, Natalie J., and Susan C. Pearce. "Locking Up Hope: Immigration, Gender, and the Prison System." *Scholar and Feminist Online* 6, no. 3 (2008). https://sfonline .barnard.edu/immigration/sokoloff_pearce_01.htm.

Song, Charles, and Suzy Lee. "Between a Sharp Rock and a Very Hard Place: The Trafficking Victims Protection Act and the Unintended Consequences of the Law Enforcement Cooperation Requirement." *Intercultural Human Rights Law Review* 1 (2006): 133–56.

Spade, Dean. "Intersectional Resistance and Law Reform: Intersectionality; Theorizing Power, Empowering Theory." *Signs: Journal of Women in Culture and Society* 38, no. 4 (2013): 1031–55.

Spade, Dean. *Mutual Aid: Building Solidarity During This Crisis (and the Next)*. Versa, 2020.

Spade, Dean. *Normal Life: Administrative Violence, Critical Trans Politics, and the Limits of Law*. South End, 2011.

Spade, Dean, and Craig Willse. "Confronting the Limits of Gay Hate Crimes Activism: A Radical Critique." *Chicano Latino Law Review* 21 (2000): 38–52.

Spivak, Gayatri Chakravorty. *Can the Subaltern Speak? Reflections on the History of an Idea*. Edited by Rosalind C. Morris. Columbia University Press, 2010.

Stanley, Eric A. *Atmospheres of Violence: Structuring Antagonism and the Trans/Queer Ungovernable*. Duke University Press, 2021.

Stoever, Jane K. *The Politicization of Safety: Critical Perspectives on Domestic Violence Responses*. NYU Press, 2019.

Suchland, Jennifer. *Economies of Violence: Transnational Feminism, Postsocialism, and the Politics of Sex Trafficking*. Duke University Press, 2015.

Swavola, Elizabeth, Kristine Riley, and Ram Subramanian. *Overlooked: Women and Jails in an Era of Reform*. Vera Institute of Justice, 2016. https://www.vera.org/downloads /publications/overlooked-women-and-jails-report-updated.pdf.

Thuma, Emily L. *All Our Trials: Prisons, Policing, and the Feminist Fight to End Violence*. University of Illinois Press, 2019.

Trinh, T. Minh-ha. "Not You/Like You: Post-Colonial Women and the Interlocking Questions of Identity and Difference." *Inscriptions* 3/4 (1988): 71–76.

Trinh, T. Minh-ha. *Woman, Native, Other: Writing Postcoloniality and Feminism*. Indiana University Press, 1989.

Tuck, Eve. "Suspending Damage: A Letter to Communities." *Harvard Educational Review* 79, no. 3 (2009): 409–28.

Tuck, Eve, and K. Wayne Yang. "What Justice Wants." *Critical Ethnic Studies* 2, no. 2 (2016): 1–15.

US Citizenship and Immigration Services. *Characteristics of T Nonimmigrant Status (T Visa) Applicants Fact Sheet*. 2022. https://www.uscis.gov/sites/default/files /document/fact-sheets/Characteristics_of_T_Nonimmigrant _Status_TVisa_Applicants_FactSheet_FY08_FY22.pdf.

US Citizenship and Immigration Services. "Green Card for VAWA Self-Petitioner." Last modified May 22, 2025. https://www.uscis.gov/green-card/green-card-eligibility /green-card-for-vawa-self-petitioner.

US Citizenship and Immigration Services. *Trends in U Visa Law Enforcement Certifications, Qualifying Crimes, and Evidence of Helpfulness: Analysis of Data Through FY 2018*. July 2020. https://www.uscis.gov/sites/default/files/document/reports/U _Visa_Report-Law_Enforcement_Certs_QCAs_Helpfulness.pdf.

US Citizenship and Immigration Services. *U Visa Demographics: Analysis of Data Through FY 2019*. March 2020. https://www.uscis.gov/sites/default/files/document /reports/U_Visa_Report_-_Demographics.pdf.

US Citizenship and Immigration Services. *U Visa Filing Trends: Analysis of Data Through FY 2019*. April 2020. https://www.uscis.gov/sites/default/files/document /reports/Mini_U_Report-Filing_Trends_508.pdf.

US Citizenship and Immigration Services. "Victims of Criminal Activity: U Nonimmigrant Status." Last modified May 16, 2025. https://www.uscis.gov/humanitarian /victims-of-criminal-activity-u-nonimmigrant-status.

US Citizenship and Immigration Services. "Victims of Human Trafficking: T Nonimmigrant Status." Last modified May 16, 2025. https://www.uscis.gov/humanitarian /victims-of-human-trafficking-t-nonimmigrant-status.

US Department of Health and Human Services. *Services Available to Victims of Human Trafficking: A Resource Guide for Social Service Providers*. May 2012.

US Department of Health and Human Services, Administration for Children and Families. "Programs to Reduce Human Trafficking Receive $2 Million." May 6, 2009. https://www.acf.hhs.gov/archive/media/press/2009/programs-reduce-human -trafficking-receive-2-million.

US Department of Health and Human Services, Administration for Children and Families. "Testimony on ACF Activities Under Trafficking Victims Protection Act of 2000." June 8, 2004. https://www.acf.hhs.gov/archive/testimony/testimony-acf -activities-under-trafficking-victims-protection-act-2000.

US Department of Health and Human Services, Administration for Children and Families, Office of Refugee Resettlement. "Anti-Trafficking in Persons Programs." Last modified April 23, 2019. https://www.acf.hhs.gov/archive/orr/programs/ anti-trafficking/about.

US Department of Homeland Security. "U and T Visa Law Enforcement Resource Guide for Federal, State, Local, Tribal and Territorial Law Enforcement, Prosecutors,

Judges, and Other Government Agencies." January 2019. https://asistahelp.org
/wp-content/uploads/2019/08/DHS-U-and-T-Visa-Law-Enforcement-Resource
-Guide.pdf.

US Department of Homeland Security, Citizenship and Immigration Services, Office of Performance and Quality. "Number of Form I-918, Petition for U Nonimmigrant Status, by Fiscal Year, Quarter, and Case Status, Fiscal Years 2009–2020." 2022. https:// www.uscis.gov/sites/default/files/document/data/I918u_visastatistics_fy2020_qtr1 .pdf.

US Department of Homeland Security, Citizenship and Immigration Services, Office of Performance and Quality. "Number of Form I-914, Application for T Nonimmigrant "Status, by Fiscal Year, Quarter, and Case Status, Fiscal Years 2008–2023." 2023. https:// www.uscis.gov/sites/default/files/document/data/i914t_visastatistics_fy2023_qtr3 .pdf.

US Department of Justice, Office of Community Oriented Policing Services. *Enhancing Community Policing with Immigrant Populations*. 2008. https://www.sheriffs.org/ sites/default/files/cops-w0747-pub.pdf.

US Department of State. *Establishment of the Human Smuggling and Trafficking Center: A Report to Congress*. June 16, 2005. https://2009-2017.state.gov/documents /organization/49600.pdf.

US House of Representatives, Subcommittee on Immigration and Claims. *Battered Immigrant Women Protection Act of 1999: Hearing on HR 3083*, 106th Cong., 2nd Sess., July 20, 2000.

US Senate, Committee on Foreign Relations. *Hearing on the Global Fight to End Modern Slavery*, 115th Cong., 2nd Sess., November 28, 2018.

Visweswaran, Kamala. *Fictions of Feminist Ethnography*. University of Minnesota Press, 1994.

Volpp, Leti. "Blaming Culture for Bad Behavior." *Yale Journal of Law and the Humanities* 12, no. 1 (2000): 89–116.

Volpp, Leti. "The Citizen and the Terrorist." *Critical Race Studies* 49, no. 5 (2002): 1575–600.

Volpp, Leti. "Framing Cultural Difference: Immigrant Women and Discourses of Tradition." *Differences* 22, no. 1 (2011): 90–110.

Volpp, Leti. "(Mis)Identifying Culture: Asian Women and the 'Cultural Defense.'" *Harvard Women's Law Journal* 17 (1994): 57–101.

Walia, Harsha. *Undoing Border Imperialism*. AK Press, 2013.

Wang, Lee Ann S. "Unsettling Innocence: Rewriting the Law's Invention of Immigrant Woman as Cooperator and Criminal Enforcer." *Scholar and Feminist Online* 13, no. 2 (2016). https://sfonline.barnard.edu/lee-ann-wang-unsettling-innocence-rewriting -the-laws-invention-of-immigrant-woman-as-cooperator-and-criminal-enforcer/.

Washington State Coalition Against Domestic Violence. "Moment of Truth: Statement of Commitment to Black Lives." June 30, 2020. https://wscadv.org/news/moment-of -truth-statement-of-commitment-to-black-lives/.

Weheliye, Alexander G. *Habeas Viscus: Racializing Assemblages, Biopolitics, and Black Feminist Theories of the Human*. Duke University Press, 2014.

Williams, Patricia J. *The Alchemy of Race and Rights*. Harvard University Press, 1991.

Winston, Celeste. *How to Lose the Hounds: Maroon Geographies and a World Beyond Policing*. Duke University Press, 2023.

Yngvesson, Barbara, and Susan Coutin. "Schrödinger's Cat and the Ethnography of Law." *Political and Legal Anthropology Review* 31, no. 1 (2008): 61–78.

Young, Hershini Bhana. *Illegible Will: Coercive Spectacles of Labor in South Africa and the Diaspora*. Duke University Press, 2017.

Index

Against Women Act (VAWA), 12, 35, 111n16. *See also* gender-based violence; sexual violence; violence against women

Escobar, Martha, 16
Esmeir, Samera, 108n15
ethnic studies, 7, 37, 83, 92
ethnography, 42; feminist, 43–44; impasses of, 22, 24, 29–30, 34, 39–41, 48, 50, 56, 63; legal, 6, 18–24, 28, 35, 43, 72, 109n30; refusal in, 18, 31–32, 37
evidence of experience, 20, 28
exceptionalism, 31, 49, 54, 59–60, 63, 84, 107–8n83; Asian American, 96
exclusion, 6, 9, 14–15, 21, 30, 35, 38, 47, 58

failure to protect laws, 10
Farley, Anthony, 8, 104n18
FBI Law Enforcement Bulletin, 52–53, 110n13
Federal Bureau of Investigation (FBI), 76, 87–88
felt theory, 32
feminism, 7, 20, 24, 28–29, 31–32, 38, 74, 77, 79, 89; antiviolence movements, 18, 78, 94, 105n34; Asian American, 3, 18, 34–35, 37, 39, 93; Black, 18; in carceral reforms, 96; ethnography and, 43–44; humanitarian projects, 104n9; Indigenous, 5, 108n7; transnational, 70, 108n3; white, 5, 36, 78, 108n7; women of color and, 6, 11, 17, 23, 43, 50, 65, 70, 72, 93–95. *See also* abolition feminism
Ferreira da Silva, Denise, 21, 38
fetishization of safety, 11
Finley, Chris, 6
Floyd, George, 104n10
Fukushima, Annie, 86
funding, 28, 42, 55; antitrafficking, 72–75, 79, 82, 84, 86–87, 113n18, 113n28; categories, 3, 12; de-, 5, 93, 95; law enforcement, 2–3, 8, 10, 12–13, 48–49, 66, 93, 105n41, 111n16; for prisons, 13

Garcia, Romina, 8
Gehi, Pooja, 65, 96
gender, 9–10, 13, 15, 32–34, 61, 64, 74, 95; immigration and, 76–77, 85; law and, 6, 22,

36–37, 58, 65, 81, 109n21; policing of, 20, 34, 48; victimhood and, 17, 28, 31, 36; Violence Against Women Act (VAWA) provisions and, 35, 47, 49, 70, 72, 104n14
gender-based violence, 10–11, 20, 22–23, 27, 46, 49, 54–55, 58, 85, 89; Asian American politics and, 8, 35; exceptionalizing of, 31; feminist critiques of, 18, 38; incarceration and, 3–5, 18; policing and, 1, 60; race and, 25, 66; state violence and, 44, 50. *See also* domestic violence; sexual violence; violence against women
gender studies, 7
Georgis, Dina, 28
Gersten, Christopher, 84
Gilmore, Ruth Wilson, 8, 60, 96, 114n9
Goodmark, Leigh, 5
Gottschalk, Marie, 12
green cards, 55, 60–61, 71, 87, 106n53
Gustafson, Kaaryn, 13, 85, 114n41

Haley, Sarah, 8
Han, Sora, 21–22, 34–35, 37–38, 108n12
Hanhardt, Christina, 49
Haritaworn, Jin, 58
harm, 2–4, 10–11, 46, 54, 57, 66, 72, 76–77, 79, 89, 104n15; accountability and, 49, 67, 93–94; cooperation and, 7, 112n12; detaching from care, 98; of law, 22; proving, 38, 56; reducing, 88, 93–94; reproducing, 37, 74
Harris, Cheryl, 9, 104–5n22
Hartman, Saidiya, 29, 33, 97
hate crimes, 92–96
heteropatriarchy, 3, 28, 31
Hill, Annie, 80, 86
homonormativity, 20, 58, 93
Hong, Grace, 34, 93
Hua, Julietta, 86
humanitarianism, 5–6, 11, 14, 20, 28, 36, 40, 86, 110n2; feminist, 104n9; imperial, 4, 17; militarized, 17, 60, 73–74
humanity, 9, 33, 35, 70, 77, 108n15
humanization, 9, 36, 38, 59, 66
Hunt, Sarah, 80
Hwang, Ren-yo, 96

Illegal Immigration Reform and Immigrant Responsibility Act (IIRIRA), 15–16

www.ingramcontent.com/pod-product-compliance
Lightning Source LLC
Chambersburg PA
CBHW030852270326
41928CB00008B/1332